T0382527

THE LAWS OF VERSE

THE LAWS OF VERSE

BY

JOHANNES C. ANDERSEN
F.N.Z.Inst.

Is there a reason in metre?
Give us your speech, master Peter!
R. Browning, *King Francis*

CAMBRIDGE
AT THE UNIVERSITY PRESS
MCMXXVIII

CAMBRIDGE
UNIVERSITY PRESS

University Printing House, Cambridge CB2 8BS, United Kingdom

Published in the United States of America by Cambridge University Press, New York

Cambridge University Press is part of the University of Cambridge.

It furthers the University's mission by disseminating knowledge in the pursuit of education, learning and research at the highest international levels of excellence.

www.cambridge.org
Information on this title: www.cambridge.org/9781107690974

© Cambridge University Press 1928

First published 1928
First paperback edition 2014

A catalogue record for this publication is available from the British Library

ISBN 978-1-107-69097-4 Paperback

To

THE LATE
T. S. OMOND

whose criticism I valued much
and whose friendship I valued more

CONTENTS

PREFACE

I WAS first introduced to the science of prosody by R. F. Brewer, B.A., through his *Orthometry, A Treatise on the Art of Versification*, 1893; and I remember that, having read the book, I was convinced that much had been left unsaid; the analysis was not sufficiently exhaustive.

From Brewer I turned to other prosodists mentioned in his bibliography, though few of their works were here in the Antipodes. In course of time, however, I became acquainted, through his books, with the late T. S. Omond, and in 1908 I began a correspondence with him which continued until the time of his regretted death in 1923. I wrote to him because it seemed to me that of prosodists then living his theory of the structure of verse came nearest the truth. I cannot speak too highly of his kindness and courtesy at all times in writing, and in debating points of difference, and he warned me that as regards prosody I had entered "a fair field full of fighting folk." I could wish that my theory, the moulding of which bears some impress of his hand, had been published during his lifetime. Now I can but dedicate it to his memory. He sent me in February 1909 a copy of his *English Metrists* of 1907, and from this book I was able to glean something of the theories of writers whose works I was unable to secure.

In the body of the present book I have mentioned several of the prosodists whose theories, at one time, or still widely accepted, appear at least in part to run counter to my theory; but I have not mentioned all whose writings I have studied, nor does it seem necessary to do so.

Guided by the laws set out in the following pages, it is possible to classify all accentual poetry as certainly as plants or animals can be classified. It seems natural that this should be possible, seeing that poetry, too, is a living growth; not an artificial product.

There appears to be a yet deeper law, not touched in this volume. I believe that Proserpina, roaming the gleaming fields of Enna, heard the faint far music on which the flowers she gathered were thrilled to shape and colour; and that the same music, in other Protean form, thrills to shape the flowers of thought in the fields of the imagination. The music beats in us all; a few are able to give it voice and expression; we others can but hear and wonder.

J. C. A.

NEW ZEALAND
    December, 1927

CHAPTER I

FORMAL CHARACTERISTICS
OF POETRY

THE essential difference between prose and poetry is not in matter, but in mechanism; not in the loftiness or beauty of expression, but in the method of giving utterance to that loftiness or beauty. Unless the matter is presented on the page in a different way, the reader is at first unable to say if prose or poetry is intended. If written continuously across the page it will be assumed that prose is intended; if written in short lines of comparatively regular length it will be assumed that poetry is intended, and the two readings will be quite different. If read aloud, however, the listener is at once able to decide if prose or poetry is intended.

The following words will serve as an example:

It was of a strange order, that the doom of these two creatures should be thus traced out almost like reality—the one to end in madness—both in misery.

This passage would unhesitatingly be read as prose; yet it forms the concluding paragraph of *The Dream*, by Byron. The difference will be more marked if the words be read aloud. Supposing the reader, having read it as prose, were shewn it as poetry:

It was of a strange order, that the doom
Of these two creatures should be thus traced out
Almost like reality—the one
To end in madness—both in misery.

Then, on reading it again with that knowledge, he would read it in quite a different way, with a certain lilt or beat. Were it actually prose, and he tried to read it with the lilt or beat, he would halt and stumble continually.

With this in mind, how would the following extracts be read, supposing the reader did not know from whence they were taken?

> ...suddenly the gladsome light leaped over hill and valley, casting amber, blue, and purple, and a tint of rich red rose, according to the scene they lit on, and the curtain flung around; yet all alike dispelling fear and the cloven hoof of darkness, all on the wings of hope advancing, and proclaiming, "God is here." Then life and joy sprang reassured from every crouching hollow; every flower, and bud, and bird, had a fluttering sense of them; and all the flashing of God's gaze merged into soft beneficence. So perhaps shall break upon us that eternal morning, when crag and chasm shall be no more, neither hill and valley, nor great unvintaged ocean;...

and again,

> Thel answered: "O thou little virgin of the peaceful valley, giving to those that cannot crave, the voiceless, the o'ertired, thy breath doth nourish the innocent lamb; he smells thy milky garments, he crops thy flowers, whilst thou sittest smiling in his face..."

Being printed as prose, both extracts will no doubt be read as prose, though a vagrant lilt will assert itself, especially in the first:

So perhaps shall break upon us that eternal morning,
When crag and chasm shall be no more, neither hill and valley,
Nor great unvintaged ocean;...

The first extract is, however, from a prose work, Blackmore's *Lorna Doone*; the second from a poem, Blake's *The Book of Thel*.

What actually is the lilt that seems to assert itself immediately the matter is perceived to be poetry, or is assumed to be poetry? What is it that causes the lilt?

The lilt is as essential to blank and other five-beat verse as it is to lyric, but it is more pronounced in lyric; and as certain metrical laws may be deduced from lyric poetry, the examples here used will be drawn chiefly from lyric sources.

The lilt of the following words cannot be suppressed by giving them the guise of prose:

> There blew a drowsy, drowsy wind, deep sleep upon me fell,
> the Queen of Fairies she was there and took me to hersell.
>
> *Tamlane*, st. 18.

These words appear almost mechanically to arrange themselves, two words of like sound dividing them into two equal portions:

> There blew a drowsy, drowsy wind, deep sleep upon me fell,
> The Queen of Fairies she was there and took me to hersell.

Supposing the order of the words to have been "A drowsy, drowsy wind blew, deep sleep fell upon me, the Queen of Fairies was there and took me to hersell," there would have been no suggestion of lilt, or even division of the whole sentence into two portions; the rhythm has been changed, the metre has been destroyed. It was not the order of the words that made them poetry, it was the metre desired that caused their unproselike order. Such transpositions as "deep sleep upon me fell" instead of "deep sleep fell upon me" are exceedingly common in poetry. It is not the transposition that makes the poetry, however, but the metre that necessitates the transposition. The metre is something apart from the words, though it needs sound to reveal its presence.

Since the two long lines above are metrical, there must be something in them that can be measured. It has already been seen that they appear naturally to divide as printed. There is a further division, as is indicated by the way in which lines such as the above are usually printed:

> There blew a drowsy, drowsy wind,
>   Deep sleep upon me fell,
> The Queen of Fairies she was there
>   And took me to hersell.

Supposing the second line to be written "Deep sleep fell upon me," the regularity is disturbed; the manner of the recurrence of the accents has been changed. The metre seems to depend, in some way, on the regular recurrence of the accents; and it is evident that in the above the accents occur with almost perfect regularity:

> There blèw a dròwsy, dròwsy wìnd,
>   Dèep slèep upòn me fèll,
> The Quèen of Faìries shè was thère
>   And tòok me tò hersèll.

It is now, too, evident why the redundant 'she' was inserted in the third line; it makes accentually regular an otherwise irregular line.

The first apparent cause of the regularity is the alternation of unaccented and accented syllables, but that this is not the only cause is evident when it is seen that the words 'deep sleep' both bear accents, and the word 'to' in the fourth line bears only a fictitious accent.

Now will be seen the reason for the metrical nature of the lines from *Lorna Doone*:

> So perhaps shall break upon us
>   That eternal morning,
> When crag and chasm shall be no more,
>   Neither hill and valley,

There is here a perfect regularity of accents, though the first accent in each of three of the lines is not preceded by an unaccented syllable and the last accent in the same lines is followed by an unaccented syllable.

It is evident then that in this regularity the accented syllables may be either preceded by unaccented syllables, as in line three above, or succeeded by them, as in lines one, two, and four. Supposing the first line were to be printed, "Perhaps shall break upon us so," then lines one and three have the same rhythm, and lines two and four the same, the former starting with unaccented syllables, the latter with accented. A difference, however, appears at the end of the first line, a difference more noticeable when the full verse of two lines is printed:

So perhaps shall break upon us that eternal morning,

and

Perhaps shall break upon us so   that eternal morning,

Here a decided break, or pause, or hover, occurs in the second printing that does not occur in the first; a break similar to the one in the following full verse:

When crag and chasm shall be no more,   neither hill and valley,

The pause before 'that,' which should rather be regarded as a hover on the vowel of 'so' since there is no actual cessation of sound, or very little, is evidently brought about because the preceding unaccented syllable has disappeared. The hover disappears if the 'so' be made 'slowly.'

Perhaps shall break upon us slowly that eternal morning,

Or the place of 'so' may be taken by 'glowingly':

Perhaps shall break upon us glowingly that eternal morning,

It would appear, then, that each accented syllable is accompanied by one or more unaccented syllables, or in their absence by an equivalent hover; a hover into which one or more syllables may be inserted, the hover disappearing on their insertion. Should the accented syllable be dropped instead of the unaccented, the hover still occurs:

I hànker   and cànker   to sèe their cùrsed prìde.

A syllable may take the place of the hover:

I hànker màir and cànker sàir to sèe...

or two syllables:

I hànker the màir and cànker is sàir to sèe...

Syllables, apparently, are not of the importance they at first seemed to be; but if they are dropped, something takes their place. This something, indeed, was there the whole time: it was created once the syllables and their arrangement gave the cue to its existence. A rhythm of time underlies the words, and once this rhythm has been perceived, syllables can be omitted or inserted, accents suppressed, up to a certain point, without the perception of that rhythm being lost. It is this rhythm of time that is metrical, and to it the words are accommodated. It flows as it were in regular waves, the accented syllables, when present, coinciding with the crests of the waves, the passing of the wave-crest being felt even when syllables are absent. The full verses so far considered may be shewn diagrammatically floating on the time-waves:

Sò perhàps shall brèak upòn us thàt   etèrnal mòrning,
I hànker   and cànker   to sèe their cùrsed prìde.

In the second verse, the hover during which the second and fourth crests pass may look too great; but if the syllables above suggested be inserted, it will be found that the hover is not too great; is not so great as it seems to be. It will be noted that every accented syllable is on a crest, every unaccented syllable in a trough of the underlying rhythm, which will be called the temporal metre. It is this metre which differentiates poetry from prose; it is always present in the former, never in the latter.

When it is said that poetry is metrical, it is the temporal metre that is measured. As will be seen later, the full verse of lyric poetry contains eight waves of the temporal metre, the full verse being usually divided into two lines of four waves each.

It will be seen, too, that accents may occur on syllables which are over the trough, not on the crest, of the temporal metre; but if an accented syllable comes in this position, another follows on the crest, and be-cause of its position on the crest the latter is always instinctively made the stronger of the two. The lines have their grammatical accents, and the coincidence of these accents with the wave-crests will for convenience be called stresses. Each full verse is palpably divided into eight parts; these will be called units; and since the stress is usually the governing feature, they will be called stress-units.

Prosodists have accepted the linear division of poetry as given instinctively, or capriciously, by individual poets, without enquiring whether the poets were guided, unconsciously or otherwise, by some most insistent yet unobtrusive law which, whilst it allows almost an infinity of variation, yet demands that every variation shall conform to a fundamental principle.

Accepting the line as written by poets, or as set up by printers, Dr Guest proposed to divide British poetry into units according to the fall of the pauses that divide a line into two or more separable, though not separate, parts. This division, however, is syntactical rather than metrical, and has already been rejected by both poets and prosodists.

A somewhat different division has been proposed by Robert Bridges. He would group together syllables that appear to belong naturally to a certain stress, so that in the same line the various stresses may control a varying number of syllables, which matters little, and their time-values be quite unequal, which matters a great deal. Thus the line

Brightest and best of the sons of the morning

he considers to be composed of the four units:

Brightest　and best　of the sons　of the morning.

This theory appears similar to the Law of Mono-pressures, adopted by the late Professor Skeat, but it is no more than a further subdividing of Guest's subdivision, and is equally applicable to prose. A metrical subdivision is one that can be applied to poetry only, exclusive altogether of prose.

Bridges's first rule of what he calls "stress prosody" is, "The stress governs the rhythm." By rhythm he presumably means metre; and it will be seen that whilst the stress indicates the metre, it by no means governs it. The error of his first law is carried on in its corollary— "The stresses must all be true speech stresses." He holds the "admitting of conventional stresses" to be a mistake, and would have the monotony of the stresses always falling regularly varied by "inverting some of the stresses, or leaving them bare," as in:

> Ìs the nìght chìlly and dàrk?
> The nìght is chìlly but nòt dàrk.

But here no note has been taken of the pauses,—unavoidable pauses or hovers, though not ineradicable,—if the stresses as marked be made in the enunciation of these words. A pause or hover appears between the words 'night' and 'chilly,' 'not' and 'dark.' Read aloud, the effect is:

> Is the night   chilly and dark?
> The night is chilly but not   dark.

The stresses have not been displaced by inversion or otherwise; they are in their natural positions, the pauses or hovers taking the place of syllables. Inserted syllables will perhaps more readily reveal the existence of the hovers:

> Is the night then chilly and dark?
> The night is chilly but not so dark.

Variation is produced, not by a displacement of the stresses, but by varying the number of syllables in the stress-units, and by varying or suppressing the stresses themselves.

The slight internal pauses or hovers in verse have no value for purposes of classification: they are of much more frequent occurrence than might on first thought be supposed; and the lighter or phonetically purer the syllables are, the more room there is for these hovers. Their appearance is, however, altogether irregular; nor is this irregularity a blemish, but the reverse.

It was the principal clausal pause that influenced Guest in making his sectional units: it is the minor syntactical pauses that has influenced Bridges in formulating his stress-units. But it must be remembered that in poetry it is not the words, and it is not the accents of the words, that create the metre; the words and accents float upon the metre, as in a series of detached or semi-detached verbal islets, linked up with sound. If the islets be isolated and classified according to their individual constituents, no doubt a certain definite number of varying units may be classified, but the verse will not have been analyzed, since no account has been taken of the metre from which the words have been lifted. It is not only the words or word-groups that are to be analyzed, but also the metre in which they float and sing; else in what respect does verse differ from prose?

The term "stress-unit" has been adopted for denoting the smallest metrical unit; but whereas Bridges's stress-units are measurements from trough to trough of the metrical wave, or rather between uncertain places upon the wave-sides, the units in the present treatise are measurements from stress to stress, from wave-crest to wave-crest; and as it is not the words themselves that are measured, there may be an overrunning of sound; that is, the metrical unit and the verbal unit that reveals it may not always be coincipient or coterminous.

Professor Saintsbury rejects Guest's sections, rejects Bridges's units, indeed, rejects all systems hitherto proposed, and formulates another, which he calls "equivalence"; that is a trochee, or a spondee, or a pyrrhic, or an anapest, may take the place of an iamb; certain "feet" are interchangeable. These interchangeable feet must be of the same "prosodic value"; but one reads and re-reads his volumes in vain for any definition of this prosodic value, or how it is to be determined. He never definitely says so, but one is driven to conclude that his prosodic value is a temporal one; for he speaks of a pause-foot or half-foot, "the equivalent of silence," as a foot "by no means impossible or unknown...in English poetry." He even admits that a foot may contain no sound at all; but he does not say what then makes it a foot. From his scansions, however, it is perfectly evident that he has temporal unity in his thoughts.

Speaking of Patmore, he says, "that he also insisted on, if he did not invent, the 'isochronous interval,' is none of my objections to him. I believe in it myself; though as I formerly pointed out (Vol. I, p. 82, note) I prefer to economise letters and call it a 'foot'" (Vol. III, pp. 439–40). The fact is, he considers the matter of what actually constitutes a foot to be beyond the scope of his enquiry.

The writer who most definitely dealt with and explained this temporal unit was T. S. Omond. "If syllables do not recur with regularity," says he, "we must fall back on that which underlies these—on the time-spaces or periods of duration in which syllables are, as it were, embedded. All verse is conditioned by time. The term 'period' may be conveniently used to denote the unit of time (less intelligibly styled a 'foot') whose constitution we are about to consider...if time govern metre—which no critic will deny—there must be units of time, and the very definition of rhythm suggests that these units are equal."

They are not absolutely equal, as Mr Omond himself shews; but once their approximate equality is perceived, their varying fluctuation, according to matter and mood, hovers perfectly about an average.

The supposed absolute equality misled Sidney Lanier in his musical scansion. He made the temporal units, the "feet," actual bars, restoring definite quantity to iambs and trochees. Poetry, however, by no means has the regularity of music; and whilst an iamb may be, and often is, short-long in actual quantity, it as often is not; and the trochee may be, but more often is not, long-short in quantity. Whilst the musical element certainly enters largely into poetry, musical scansion leads to erroneous results.

It is probable enough that the terms "isochronous interval," "period," "foot," and "stress-unit" as proposed by the present writer, are all intended to signify one and the same prosodic fact: it is merely the constitution of the unit that is in disagreement. It may even be that the users of the different terms are actually in agreement as to the constitution of the unit, but words, which in use often display an exasperating perversity, cloud the issue.

The stress-unit is the smallest recurring measureable period in metrical composition, and next to it is the verse, with its half-verse or line. This is composed of a certain definite number of stress-units, or their temporal equivalents of silence, or pause. In lyric verse,—that is in all verse excepting heroic and blank, or five-stressed verse,—the number of stress-units in each full verse is eight. The verse is usually printed in two equal parts, sometimes in more than two; and it is to these fractional parts of a full verse that the term "line" will be restricted.

The full verse is of various kinds, the simplest form being that in which it is not broken by a mid-rime,—

She's mounted on her milk-white steed, and she's ta'en Thomas
  up behind;

This verse is called a Romance verse, and verses so written are in Romance metre. Usually there is a mid-rime, when the verse naturally falls into two parts; and for convenience in printing it usually is divided into two parts whether there is a mid-rime or not.

      She's mounted on her milk-white steed,
      And she's ta'en Thomas up behind;

      As I was walking all alane,
      I heard twa corbies making a mane:

In many instances the last unit of the second line is dropped, when a Ballad verse results, in Ballad metre:

      It fell about the Martinmas,
        When nights are lang and mirk,

In addition to the last unit of the second line, half of the last unit of the first line may be dropped: the result is a Nibelungen verse, in Nibelungen metre:

      From Greenland's icy mountains,
        From India's coral strand,

or the whole of the last unit of the first line and the last unit of the second may be dropped, the result being an Alexandrine verse, in Alexandrine metre:

      My silks and fine array,
        My smiles and languished air,

In every instance, where a unit or part of a unit has been dropped, a pause takes its place, so that the time-value of the Alexandrine verse is practically the same as the time-value of the Romance verse.

These four varieties form the basis on which all lyric verse is built. Their relation to one another, and the variations to which all are subject, are fully discussed in a later chapter.

The next definite recurring period is the stanza. This is composed of any number of verses, from two upwards, the normal number being two or four. The number is definite within certain limits, but does not appear to be subject to such absolute laws as those that govern the stress-unit and the verse-unit.

CHAPTER II

THE STRESS-UNIT

THE stress-unit is the smallest regularly-recurring period in a verse of poetry. It may be altogether silent, or it may contain from one to four·syllables, or even five.

> Thou sent'st/me late/a heart/was crowned,/
> I took/it to/be thine;/

This is the way in which a verse is usually divided into its component units, it being understood, when each unit is accented on the second syllable, the first being unaccented, that the verse is composed of iambs. Clearly, however, the word "to" in the second line is not accented, so that the unit is not a Greek iamb. It is a pyrrhic, a two-syllabled unit without accent; and because of its occurrence in iambic lines prosodists have said that a pyrrhic may take the place of an iamb. Similarly, should the first line read

> Thou sent'st/me of late/a heart/was crowned,/

the second unit contains three syllables, instead of two, the third syllable accented,—an anapaest; and again, prosodists have said that an anapaest may take the place of an iamb. The rhythm is a little changed by these substitutions, but the metre remains the same. So, too, were the line altered,

> Thou sen/test me/a heart/was crowned,/

here the first unit has had part removed, yet its value remains the same. Evidently then, the syllabic stuff of the units may be altered, may be lessened or increased, without change in the metre, though with a certain amount

of change in the rhythm or music. It is the underflowing
temporal metre that makes these changes possible, and
the divisions of this metre are only approximately indicated in the usual divisions as shewn above. It is
preferred to shew these divisions as follows:

> Thou sènt'st me làte a hèart was cròwned,
>
> I tòok it to be thìne;

The mark above the vowel denotes the syntactical
accent, and the mark below it denotes the metrical
wave-crest; the combination of the two marks, è, denotes the metrical stress. It is now seen that, whilst 'to'
bears no syntactical accent, it is at the place where the
wave-crest of the temporal rhythm passes:

> I tòok it to be thìne;

The stress-marks have some analogy to the bars in
music; they divide the phrases into small comparatively
equal units;—equal temporally, but not necessarily in
the number or weight of the syllables they contain. The
stress-points are always present, though the words that
occur at their incidence may bear no syntactical accent:
the passing of the crest of the temporal wave at the
stress-point can always be felt by the reader, and this it is
that keeps the metre regular though the rhythm floating
upon it may vary, through accents being dropped or
multiplied, syllables being added or taken away.

Whilst the stress-marks act as bars, the syllables
contained between them are by no means as regular
in their values as the notes of music; there is continual
variation, not only in the duration of the syllables
themselves, but also in the time-spaces, the pauses

between the words of which the syllables may form part; so that, as has been pointed out, the hover on the vowel and liquid of 'sent'st' in

Thou sènt'st me làte a hèart was cròwned,

will admit of another syllable, or even of two or three syllables, in the second unit, when the hover on either 'sent'st' or 'me' is proportionately shortened.

Thou sènt'st me làte...
Thou sènt'st me of làte...
Thou sènt'st to me of làte...

or even

Thou sèntest to me of làte...

where the second units contain two, three, four, and five syllables,—and examples of such units may be found in the best poets, though hurried units such as the five-syllabled one are very rare.

In these examples the value of each individual syllable is palpably altered; nor need the individual syllables be of the same value. The values of the syllables in the second example may be:

Thou sènt'st mĕ ŏf lāte...

or

Thou sènt'st mē ŏf lāte...

and in both instances the long syllable, marked with the –, may be more or less than equal temporally to the two short ones, and the two short ones may or may not be equally short. Again the very slight pause after 'sent'st' may vary, sometimes equalling the time-value of a short syllable; the pause may still be there even after the addition of a syllable, but in such a case the added syllable and its adjacent fellow are themselves shortened.

A   2

The values may differ, too, with different readers, or with the same reader at different times;—there is an infinity of variation. The total comparative time-value of the units, however, does not change in this way; the values of the full units are comparatively equal, however much the values of the contained syllables may vary through increase or decrease in their number or weight. This it is which differentiates the stress-unit altogether from a bar of music—which it resembles in that all units are more or less equal—and this it is which differentiates it altogether from the classic "foot."

It seems immaterial whether the stress is considered as the first element of the unit or the last. In music it is considered the first, and begins the bar, and in metre of trochaic rhythm it does appear to begin the unit. Trochaic rhythm should, however, end with an unaccented syllable; but as perhaps ninety per cent. of the rhythmic verses of British poetry end with the stressed syllable, the stress has, for convenience, been taken as ending the unit.

Units which lead up to the stress far outnumber those that begin with the stress, and these have been called ordinary units instead of iambs; those that begin with the stress have, from their nature, been called abrupt units instead of trochees. The words iamb and trochee are, however, so widely known that the writer is reluctant to discard them, and uses them, but as signifying accentual units whose short and long vary to an infinite degree, iambs not always being absolutely ◡ —́, shŏrt lōng, and trochees being as often ◡̆ – as —́ ◡, or more often. Whenever the term iamb is used, therefore, the ever-varying accentual iamb is meant, and so of the terms trochee, dactyl, anapaest, amphibrach, or other of the well-known terms. If the quantitative foot is meant, the word Greek will be prefixed—Greek iamb, Greek trochee, and so on.

It will quickly be noted that many words in a line of poetry fall into two units; this they do in any method of scansion; but in the method here adopted there seems less disruption than in the old, as is seen in the unit quoted above:

> Thou sent'st/me late/a heart/was crowned,/
> Thou sen/test me late/...

and

> Thou sènt'st me làte a hèart was cròwned,
> Thou sèntest me làte...

Other advantages of this method will appear as the work progresses.

At one time, following classical precedent, it was held that the more or less exclusive use of iambs or trochees resulted in different rhythms. It is practically impossible, however, to use one or other exclusively. Whilst their extreme forms differ, they vary so much individually and have so many qualities in common that they are now regarded as interchangeable, being extreme rhythmical forms of the same metre. They shew, however, certain qualities that have not hitherto been given due consideration.

In the usual line of iambic rhythm, as in that quoted at the beginning of the chapter, on every accented vowel there is also a variable sonant hover, a longer or shorter lengthening of the vowel sound or vowel and liquid consonant sound, so pronounced as to admit of the insertion of another syllable, when the hover may be shortened, but the temporal value of the unit is not lengthened. The hover is apparent when the word itself ends with the stressed syllable, but there is a change should the word be three-syllabled with the stress on the second syllable, or two-syllabled with the stress on the first:

And love to live in dimple sleek;

(*L'Allegro*, l. 30.)

Here the hover appears on 'love' and 'live,' but instead of appearing on the first, and accented syllable, of 'dimple,' it is transferred to the liquid following, which is neither accented nor stressed—as is shewn in the symbols:

$$\smile \; \overline{\perp} \; \smile \; \overline{\perp} \; \smile \; \smile \; - \; \perp$$

There may be two or more words in one line shewing this transfer of the hover:

And laughter holding both his sides.

The extreme difference in the value of the hovers may be shewn clearly in the words:

Merry Mary and chary Cherry
Walked in Mary's garden.

Here the values are distinctly as follows:

Merry = $\smile$ —   Cherry = $\smile$ —
Mary = $\perp$ $\smile$ chary = $\perp$ $\smile$

It is the play between these two values that gives the varying values from $\smile$ — to $\perp$ $\smile$ to trochaic units.

In many trochaic words there is this tendency to make the accented syllable short and the unaccented one long by hovering on the latter. In the words 'below' and 'bellow' the accents are on the second and first syllables respectively, but the hover or lengthening is on the second syllable in both instances:

bĕlōw   bĕllōw

This tendency exists primarily in trochaic words containing a naturally short first vowel; a long vowel usually retains the hover; this is shewn in the two trochaic words 'holly' and 'holy':

hŏllȳ   hŏlȳ

Both are accented on the first syllable, but the hover, which is on the second syllable of the first word, is on the first of the second word. The spelling is an indication of this fact.

From the making of a series of experiments, T. L. Bolton concluded that an accented sound tended to come first in a group, a longer sound last. Mr T. S. Omond, commenting on the paper dealing with these experiments, suggests that "when we attend mainly to stresses we incline to make these begin feet, but to terminate them when we attend mainly to time...." The difference will be remarked in reading aloud; the tendency is to accentuate the stress in trochaic rhythm, slipping quickly from the stress to the hover on the following syllable; to subdue the stress, and hover on the stressed syllable in iambic rhythm. It is this tendency which creates the great difference in the lilt of the two rhythms, or rather these extreme forms of rhythm in the one metre.

The hover, and its variableness, were apparent to Ruskin; and according to its duration he divided iambs into three kinds; lyric, epic, and dramatic. He himself, however, perceived variations in the three kinds; and whilst their extremes are distinct, there are so many close intermediaries, and the three are so intimate, that no arbitrary distinction is possible.

Plunket Greene, the writer on singing, saw that the same was true of Greek trochees, which he says are occasionally given an inverted time-value by composer or singer; "thus *echo*, which as a [Greek] trochee would naturally be written ♩. ♪ or ♩ ♩ is, and should be generally sung, if not written, ♪ ♩.. The same applies to *horror*, *pity*, *lily*, *yellow*…and a good many of the exclamatory trochees."

The hover is, of course, due to the temporal characteristic of the unit, and largely assists in differentiating poetry from prose. The characteristic rhythm caused by its presence or absence on the stressed syllable may be further shewn by the following:

Mŏnă, Mŏnă, whŏ is shĕ?
Mŏnnā Vănnā, whŏ is shĕ?

The proper names are trochaic in both instances; but in the first the hover tends to rest on the long 'o' of 'Mona'; and if that word be repeated several times in succession, one notes with a shock of surprise that the words repeated are not "Mōnă Mōnă Mōnă Mōnă Mōnă," but "Mōn ăMōn ăMōn ăMōn ăMōn ă"; that is, the hover actually seems to separate the two syllables of the word, and to join the second syllable of one word to the first syllable of the next. In the second example the hover is on the second syllable, not the first, and here it is a diminishing hover rather than a sustained one as in the first, with some tendency to make a pause,

so that the words, if repeated, are never anything but
"Mŏnnā Vănnā Mŏnnā Vănnā Mŏnnā Vănnā." These
two are characteristic of the iambic and trochaic
rhythms, and their mingling or opposition produces
many fine effects in the music of verse, as in

> Banners yellow, glorious, golden,
> On its roof did float and flow.

(Poe, The Haunted Palace, st. 2.)

where the hover is on the unaccented and unstressed
syllables of the first two words, on the accented and
stressed syllables of the second two; and the contrast
between the two forms of the trochaic rhythm is seen
in the first line, and between the trochaic and iambic
forms of the metre in the closing four syllables of the
two lines:

$$\breve{\cup} - \breve{\cup} - \overset{\backprime}{\perp} \cup \overset{\backprime}{\perp} \cup$$

$$\breve{\cup} \cup \overset{\backprime}{\perp} \cup \overset{\backprime}{\perp} \cup \overset{\backprime}{\perp}$$

In units containing words like 'banners' a natural
tendency is made clear; whilst there is a certain amount
of hover on the unstressed syllable, it is usually of such
a nature that it will readily shorten to admit another
syllable. Thus in

Ănd mănȳ yŏuths ănd mănȳ māids

$$\cup \breve{\cup} - \overset{\backprime}{\perp} \cup \breve{\cup} - \overset{\backprime}{\perp}$$

the hover on the second syllable of 'many' tends to be
very short; but if such units occur among units where
the hover on adjacent units is longer, there is a tendency
to add a syllable to the unit with the short syllable, so
as to avoid or lessen the longer hover:

Ănd mănȳ ă yŏuth ănd mănȳ ă māid

(L'Allegro, l. 95.)

$$\cup \breve{\cup} \cup \cup \overset{\backprime}{\perp} \cup \breve{\cup} \cup \cup \overset{\backprime}{\perp}$$

where the temporal equality of the units is secured without undue lengthening or shortening of any syllable.
Again, this results in a three-syllabled ripple, which
to some ears is objectionable when coming in rhythm
basically two-syllabled, and these would have the line
read with the 'y' and 'a' coalesced in one sound:

> And manya youth and manya maid ;

or if the ripple is brought about as in

> The làbouring clòuds do òften rèst
> ı   ı   ı   ı   (*L'Allegro*, l. 74.)

they would excise the vowel sound 'ou':

> The làbring clòuds do òften rèst
> ı   ı   ı   ı

when all units are two-syllabled, and a more uniform
rhythm results. The very essence of lyric poetry is,
however, a ceaseless varying of this uniformity—a
varying which Professor Saintsbury has aptly called
"fingering."

There are readers to whom syllabic uniformity is a
necessity; but there are others who find keen delight
in the continual varying of this uniformity:—a certain
uniformity is essential to both kinds of readers—that
is, the comparative equality temporally of the units or
feet. On the latter point apparently all prosodists are
agreed, though they may differ in their nomenclature,
and dispute unnecessarily about the nomenclature. The
point about which they actually do differ is how the
syllables are to be disposed in the units, and this is
a matter where there should be no disputation at all,
seeing it is a matter where everyone, prosodist and
reader alike, is a law to himself. So long as the temporal
units, the stress-units, are comparatively equal, the

manner of filling in of the syllables does not matter so far as prosodic law is concerned. Hence the creations of Tom D'Urfey and John Milton, whose verses are on the same fundamental principle, may exist side by side, and hence the imperceptible steps of the gradation between them. They are as the extreme colours in the spectrum of verse; and between them some choose one colour, some another, some several,—some are sufficiently eclectic to choose and find pleasure in all. There may be tumbling metre, there may be doggerel, but the calling of names does not break the common foundation. Moreover, there must always be extremes, and the wider apart these are, the wider is the range for the sweep of the pens.

The keeping of the rhythm as nearly as possible purely two-syllabled or purely three-syllabled gives the sharpest contrast of the two rhythms, but there are so many intermediate forms, so many poems where it is impossible to say if they give the two-syllabled or three-syllabled effect, that it must be admitted there is a certain Mesopotamia where the two flow and mingle and become inseparable. From this mingling welled *Christabel*, to mention only one; and throughout two-syllabled verse such lines as Milton's above will be found.

Though the ripples are heavier in the following:

> The poplars are felled ; farewell to the shade

the line is a parallel to

> And many a youth and many a maid ;

yet the former is at home in a distinctively three-syllabled poem, the latter in one distinctively two-syllabled.

As the effects of the two forms of two-syllabled rhythm, iambic and trochaic, are brought about by the position of the syntactical pauses and hovers, so the effects of the three forms of three-syllabled rhythm are brought about by the syntactical pauses and hovers.

Poe long ago shewed how intimately the three named forms are connected, quoting from Byron's *Bride of Abydos*:

> Knòw ye the lànd where the cỳpress and mỳrtle
> Are èmblems of dèeds that are dòne in their clìme?
> Where the ràge of the vùlture, the lòve of the tùrtle,
> Now melt into sorrow, now madden to crime?

Here the first three lines have been said to illustrate the three-syllabled Greek feet, dactyl, amphibrach, and anapaest.

When, however, it is remembered that the first two lines are but one full verse:

> Knòw ye the lànd where the cỳpress and mỳrtle are èmblems of dèeds that are dòne in their clìme?

it is seen that the rhythm of the second line is merely a continuation of that of the first, the slight syntactical break making the difference in the lilt. Again, did the first line open

> Do ye knòw of the lànd where the cỳpress...

the rhythm would not have been changed, yet it is the same as that of the third line.

Whilst it is not, therefore, denied that when used purely the three forms have distinct rhythmical effects, it is contended that the three are due merely to syntactical differences of arrangement; their metrical basis is the same.

Further, the unit through which the anapaest, ‿ ‿ ⊻,
lilts to the dactyl, ⊻ ‿ ‿, is the amphibrach, ‿ ⊻ ‿. In all
these the sign ⌣̇ simply means that the syllable may
have all values between short ‿ and long –.

This amphibrach, which is no more than a feminine
iamb, has already been met with in Milton's line

> And many a youth and many a maid
>
> ‿ ⌣̇ ‿ ‿ ‾ ‿ ⌣̇ ‿ ‿ ‾

Its appearing in the first and third units causes the
appearance of the three-syllabled ripple; so that besides
acting as bridge between the anapaest and the dactyl,
it also acts as bridge between the two-syllabled and
the three-syllabled rhythms.

It is here called the feminine iamb because in two-
syllabled rhythm it first makes its appearance in an
iambic word with feminine ending. Generally it appears at the line-end:

> When lòvely wòman stòops to fòlly
>
> ‿ ⌣̇ – ⌣̇ – ‾ ‿ ⌣̇ ‿

It is distinct at the end of the line, it is latent in both
the first unit and the second, appearing on the introduction of light syllables:

> How lòvely of wòman to stòop to no fòlly
>
> ‿ ⌣̇ ‿ ‿ ⌣̇ ‿ ‿ ‾ ‿ ‿ ⌣̇ ‿

The first two units now shew the feminine iamb, the
last a feminine anapaest. It should be remembered,
however, that it is a feminine iamb chiefly at the line-
end, as in the words 'to folly' above; when it occurs
within the line, the feminine ending is the first syllable
of the anapaest following.

This treatise deals chiefly with lyric poetry, but here is seen the inception of the supernumerary syllable that has caused so much discussion in theories on Blank Verse. If a feminine may appear at the end of a line or verse, why not within it? That it does so is abundantly evident; it is the feminine iamb that has caused so great clatter in the prosodic crossing of swords. The feminine iamb disturbs rhythmical uniformity; the feminine iamb confounds the distinction between the anapaest and the dactyl, between the two-syllabled rhythm and the three-syllabled; the feminine iamb is the uniter where the prosodist would have separation. In the octosyllabic couplet the feminine iamb gives a magical lift and lilt, and orders the graceful contredanse between iamb and trochee; she has been called ghost-foot; an instigator of barbaric elision; she has been called "abominable, unutterable and worse" instead of being acknowledged, as she is, a fertile source of never-ending rhythmic variety, an inexhaustible creator of prosodic beauty and grace.

In lyric, as in blank verse, there may even be the double feminine:

> But kèener thy gàze than the lìghtning's glàre,
>   And swìfter thy stèp than the èarthquake's tràmp;
> Thou dèafenest the ràge of the òcean; thy stàre
>   Makes blìnd the volcànoes...

(Shelley, Liberty, st. 3.)

Here the first units of the first and second lines contain feminine iambs, the first of the third line a double feminine. The last causes the second unit of that line to contain four syllables.

It was no doubt this intimate union of syllables on either side of a stress that caused Bridges to formulate his stress-units; but these units are due to the syntactical construction; they vary continually and infinitely. The actual unit is between stress and stress; it is the temporal unit, that varies little in duration, and seems to vary not at all, however much the syllabic burden may vary in number of syllables, in rhythmical pauses, in hovers, in hurryings. There is the regular sweep of the underflowing metre, and the irregularly disposed word-stuff floating upon it;—irregularly disposed, yet with such approach to regularity that the natural accents coincide, in most cases, with the wave-crests of the temporal metre. Thus units may be found that appear fragmentary or broken if the temporal metre be disregarded; but if that metre be remembered, it will be seen that units are composed of silence and of sound, mingled in all manner of proportions.

It has been held that two-syllabled and three-syllabled rhythms are essentially different; that one is in duple time, the other in triple time. This has been held, too, by prosodists who do not believe in musical scansion being applied to poetry.

Mr Omond quotes the following verse:

The sun, the moon, the stars, the seas, the hills,

and says—"No one, reading it, would doubt its iambic structure....Yet, if we turn to Tennyson's poem *The Higher Pantheism*, we shall find the words...followed by other three: 'and the plains.' This addition works a notable change...the time underlying the whole poem is triple."

If this be so, then surely the time underlying all

two-syllabled verse may or must be considered as triple, for all two-syllabled units have the latent power of amplification to three-syllabled. This fact, too, might warrant the comparison between accentual iambs and Greek iambs, where one long is twice the value of one short. This comparison actually is made by Lanier in his musical scansion, where he makes ordinary two-syllabled rhythm conform to short-long, using quaver-crotchet instead of $\smile -$. But there is no such inflexible unit; it varies, as has been stated, from short-short $\smile \smile$ to long-long $--$, in every rhythmic scheme. Were Lanier followed, then our two-syllabled rhythms, instead of being in duple time as most prosodists and most readers suppose, would be in triple time.

If, in Tennyson's verse above, the three-syllabled unit at its close throw a transforming spirit backward through all that goes before, making triple that which appeared duple, would not a three-syllabled unit at the opening be more powerful to transform the line following it? And with this question in mind, is Shelley's *Indian Serenade* to be regarded as in duple or triple time?

> I arise from dreams of thee
> In the first sweet sleep of night,
> When the winds are breathing low,
> And the stars are burning bright.

So too the verse

> And swims, or sinks, or wades, or creeps, or flies:

—would this be transformed to triple were the words 'in the deep' added? Even Mr Omond would hardly have said so.

It is not denied that the hover on every stressed

syllable in the two-syllabled verses quoted gives such syllables greater time-value than the unstressed syllables, but such value constantly varies, and can be denoted by no unvarying arbitrary sign; and to make duple and triple time, the signs must be constant and arbitrary.

The terms duple and triple have been taken from music; duple, or common time, the imperfect time of earlier music, containing bars whose number of beats is divisible by two, and triple time, the perfect time of earlier music, containing bars whose number of beats is divisible by three. Common (duple) time is of two kinds, simple and compound. In simple common time the bar may contain four beats, every beat being a minim equal to two crotchets, or a crotchet equal to two quavers:—that is, the number of beats in the bar is divisible by two, and the note to each beat is divisible by two. In compound common (duple) time, however, whilst the number of beats is still divisible by two, the note to each beat is divisible by three;—that is, in simple common time, or four-minim time, each minim is equal to two crotchets; in compound common time, however, each minim is dotted, and is therefore equal to three crotchets.

Supposing, then, in a bar of four minims

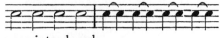

triplets were introduced,

there would be a mixture of simple and compound

time; and if all were made triplets simple time would have become compound, but would still be common (duple) time since the number of beats in the bar, four, is still divisible by two. In poetry, the full verses, and the half verses, always comprize stress-units in multiples of two; eight in the full verse, four in the half verse, exactly as in music. There is no necessity for triple time as understood in music. Neither music nor poetry is for the eye, but for the ear; arbitrary signs cannot control the rhythm;—they may indicate what the composer intended, but what the listener hears may be something quite different.

It is admitted that when the two extremes of two-syllabled rhythm and three-syllabled rhythm are compared, one may appear to be in duple time, the other in triple. The distinction loses all definiteness, however, as the comprehensive middle field is approached, the field where the two freely mingle, the field in which is found the great bulk of our virile lyric poetry.

The four-syllabled rhythm is of two kinds. In one it appears merely as a ripple in other rhythm. Thus it appears in Robert Bridges's *London Snow*:

> When men were all asleep the snow came flying,
> In large white flakes fàll*ing on the c*ìty brown,
> Stèalth*ily and perpè*tually settling and loosely lying,
> Hushing the latest tràff*ic of the dr*òwsy town;
> Deadening, muffling, stifling its murmurs failing;
> Làz*ily and incè*ssantly floating down and down;

There is a unit of four syllables, italicized, in the second verse, another in the fourth; in the third and sixth are units of five syllables. Such units are rare, and are never used as a basis for a rhythmic scheme;

they are no more than occasional variants. Similar units
appear in Swinburne's *Super flumina Babylonis*:

> By the waters of Bàbylon *we sàt* down and wept,
>> Remembering thee,
> That for ages of àgony *hast endùred*, and slept,
>> And wouldst not see.
> By the waters of Bàbylon *we stòod* up and sang,
>> Considering thee,
> That a blast of delìverance *in the dàrk*ness rang,
>> To set thee free.

In both stanzas there is a four-syllabled unit in the
first line, a five-syllabled unit in the third.

There is, however, a four-syllabled unit that is used
as the basis of a metrical scheme. It is heard in
Service's *The Lure of the Little Voices*:

> There's a cry from out the loneliness,—Oh listen, Honey, listen!
>> Do you hear it, do you fear it, you're a-holding of me so?
> You're a-sobbing in your sleep, dear, and your lashes how they
>> glisten—
>> Do you hear the Little Voices all a-begging me to go?

Is this read with the stresses coinciding with the
alternate syllables?

> There's a crỳ from òut the lònelinèss oh lìsten, Hòney, lìsten!

This may be the reading until the next line is taken,
when the unnaturalness of it is at once apparent:

> Do you hèar it, dò you fèar it, yòu're a-hòlding òf me sò?

In the first place, both lines start with a three-syllabled
unit, and if the accent on 'do' is omitted from the
first word of the second line, it should also be omitted
from the fifth word 'do.' The accent on 'of' too, is
quite unnatural,—and it is found that the alternate

accents are suppressed, making the alternate stresses
no more than minor stresses of varying degrees:

Do you hèar it, dọ you fèar it, yọu're a-hòlding ọf me sò?

The result is, that the whole stanza, instead of being
composed of verses of eight stresses is composed of
lines of four stresses with four-syllabled units; each
pair of lines, in fact, forms a normal lyric verse. Whilst
the stresses are suppressed, the resulting minor stresses
are still capable of bearing accents, as they do in the
first line:

There's a crỳ from ọut the lònelinęss oh lìsten, Họney, lìsten!

Here minor stresses are felt, if not made, at 'out' and
'Honey,' the dot below those words with the accent
marks above, ọ, representing the minor stress. It is
when the words that ride the minor stress are very
light that the two-syllabled rhythm is loosened and
becomes the four-syllabled; heavier words appear here
and there on the minor stresses as reminders of the
fact that the parent two-syllabled rhythm may at any
moment reassert itself. The words, as it were, skim
like sea-birds over the waves of the metre, never failing
to touch the alternate crests, and touching the inter-
vening ones here and there as if to be assured of their
being there should they be needed. Each four-syllabled
unit is, in fact, composed of two two-syllabled units,
in the former of which the stress is usually suppressed,
or becomes a minor stress, and in the latter of which
the stress is invariably present.

In four-syllabled rhythm, five-syllabled units may
be met, parallel in construction, but quite different in
character from those previously quoted:

The dòwnhill pàth is èasy, . come wìth me ạn it plèase ye, .

Wè *shall escàpe the ùp*hill . by nèver tỳrning bàck.

(C. Rossetti, Amor Mundi.)

Following this, the six-syllabled unit, as a coalescence of two three-syllabled units, is possible:

She has stòl'n *to the àrms of the sùm*mer, and Ì—can Ì the càll
withstànd

That has scàttered a jòy of plènteousnẹss to còv*er a blòssoming
lànd?*

There are here two six-syllabled units, as italicized,
and the second unit of the second line is five-syllabled.

The four-syllabled rhythm springs directly from the
two-syllabled. Two stanzas taken in juxtaposition will
illustrate this:

There indeed was God's own garden, sailing down the sapphire
sea—
Lawny dells and slopes of summer, dazzling stream and radiant
tree!

Out against the hushed horizon—out beneath the reverent day,
Flamed the Wonder on the waters—flamed, and flashed, and
passed away.

(Kendall, Hy-Brasil, pt. st. 2.)

If you sing of waving grasses when the plains are as dry as bricks,
And discover shining rivers where there's only mud and sticks;
If you picture 'mighty forests' where the 'mulga' spoils the view—
You're superior to Kendall, and ahead of Gordon too.

(Lawson, Australian Bards and Bush Reviewers, st. 2.)

Were the second stanza read like the first, with full
stresses on the first and every alternate syllable, it
would sound ridiculous: in it the first and every alternate stress is suppressed, or becomes a minor stress,
till something dangerously near patter is produced.
It is this danger that discounts the rhythm; yet many

poems where it forms the basis are as far removed
from patter as it is possible for poems to be; and this
end is attained, so far as mechanism is concerned, by
varying the syllabic regularity. This has been done in
Christina Rossetti's *Amor Mundi*, in George Meredith's *Love in a Valley*, in Samuel Ferguson's *The
Fairy Thorn*. It has also been done in Thackeray's
lighter verse, *The Last Buccaneer*.

The long sweep of the four-syllabled rhythm, with
the sub-flow of the two-syllabled that marks the minor
stresses, is shewn below :

There's a crỳ from òut the lòneliness—oh lìsten, Hòney, lìsten,

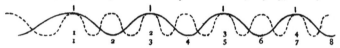

Here it will be seen that for every wave of the four-
syllabled rhythm there are two of the two-syllabled,
the crests of both coinciding at the first, third, fifth,
and seventh stresses, making these full stresses. The
two-syllabled is here a minor rhythm ; and the accents
at crests two, four, and six, that would otherwise be
full stresses, are minor stresses.

The utterance of the four-syllabled unit is inclined
to be so rapid that, unless through the dropping of
syllables, there are no hovers and no pauses such as
there are in two-syllabled and three-syllabled units.
If its speed be retarded, it is apt to resolve into the
two-syllabled units of which it is primarily composed,
the minor stresses again becoming full stresses. Its
speed may be retarded in this way mechanically by
allowing words requiring some degree of accent to
ride on the minor stresses ; the added accent converts

the minor stresses to full stresses, and the four-syllabled rhythm to two-syllabled.

The chief variations of the four-syllabled unit may be noted in a stanza of Ferguson's *The Fairy Thorn*:

They're glàncing thròugh the glìmmer o̧f the quìet . ève, .

Awày in mı̧lky wàving . of nèck and ạnkle bàre ; .

The hèavy-slı̧ding strèam . in its slèepy sò̧ng they lèave .

And the cràgs . in the ghòstly . àir.

The unit between the second and third wave-crests of the first line is the normal unit:

glì*mmer o̧f the quì*

where the three syllables preceding the one floating on the stress are unaccented, and the minor stress under 'of' is almost unnoticed. In the second unit of the line

glànc*ing thrò̧ugh the glìm*

the word 'through,' floating on the minor stress, has a certain amount of accent, and the minor stress is consequently more noticeable, as also in the second units of the second and third lines. A preponderance of units of this kind tends to clog the four-syllabled rhythm and transform it to the two-syllabled.

The third unit of the second line

wàv$\overline{ing}$. *of* nèck

drops the syllable that would have floated on the minor stress, making a unit of three syllables and a hover on 'ing.' The hover would be shortened or destroyed by the insertion of a syllable:

wàve*rı̧ng of* nèck.

The third unit of the third line also contains but three syllables, but here the hover is on the stressed word of

the second unit, an unaccented word floating on the
minor stress:

stre*am*   *in its sleep*

where the hover again would be filled, or destroyed, by
substituting 'streamlet' for 'stream.' The minor stress
may be felt either in the hover, or under the 'in.'

Two syllables, that at the minor stress and the one
following, are dropped from the last unit of the first
line, making a unit of two syllables and a hover:

qui*et*   .   *eve*

where the hover would be filled by the insertion of
'summer' between the two words.

It will be noticed that a minor stress follows the
last unit of the first line; and were the words 'of
summer time' added to that line, the hover in the last
unit would be filled by the bringing back of 'eve' to
the minor stress, and 'time' will float on the minor
stress now following 'eve'

qui*et eve of summer time   Away*

when, too, the hover bridging the space between 'eve'
and the first word of the second line, 'Away,' is almost
entirely filled, a slight syntactical pause taking its
place. So, too, the hover on 'leave' at the end of the
third line will disappear if a filling be made by substituting 'wander':

(From) the hèavy-slìding strèam ìn its slèepy sòng they wànder

And the cràgs,

The slight syntactical pause dividing the lines, if made
at all, generally causes a somewhat more hurried utterance of the words opening the next unit, so that 'and

the' is uttered in shorter time, as if to maintain the average temporal unit-length.

A very common and characteristic variation of this unit does not occur in the stanza quoted: it is seen in Gilbert's line

Of a shàrp and chìppy chòpper on a bìg blàck blòck

or in Browning's:

Sàvage Ì was sìtting ìn my hòuse làte lòne:

In the last unit an accented word floats on the minor stress, and a short hover divides the word from the stressed words on either side of it, the filling of the hovers being seen on the adding of a syllable each to 'big' and 'black'

a bìgger blàcker blòck.

The unit may be varied, and is varied, by the insertion of only one or other of such syllables:

a bìg blàcker blòck

or   a bìgger blàck blòck

and even further variations will suggest themselves:

a tèrrible blàck blòck.

The foregoing variations are quite obvious and straightforward; and it may be imagined that verses in which such an amount of variation may be employed, will result in very diverse rhythmical patterns. It may be this diversity that has caused the rhythm to be looked upon with disfavour by many; some will not see that it exists, some refuse to admit it, failing to catch the sway of it.

Apparently Francis Thompson failed. He said that the metre of *Viola* was "founded on the bold application of a metrical principle which has lain dormant since the decay of early alliterative metre...." He found "traces of it in Elizabethan poets, and from then to now it has simply dropped out of the knowledge of Englishmen." There had been a revival, he said, but an unintelligent one; Swinburne had used it beautifully, though slightly; Katharine Tynan beautifully and often. Then, speaking of that perfect poem *Love in a Valley*, he says that Meredith employed it "with the most utter and unmusical conception of its object...." He enters into details, and it is clear that he regarded it as in two-syllabled rhythm, which makes all the difference. His friend Yeats is to the point; "A poem should be a law to itself as plants and beasts are. It may be ever so finished, but all finish should merely make plain that law. Read Meredith's *Love in a Valley*. It is full of a curious, intricate richness...."

When the four-syllabled rhythm is syllabically full, it has a speed that is in danger, as has been said, of becoming patter. All units—two, three or four-syllabled—tend to one approximate time-value, the tempo being accelerated or diminished according to the spirit of the words floating upon the metre. The tempo being practically the same whichever of the three units predominates, the apparent rapidity of movement will increase, from the two-syllabled, through the three to the four-syllabled units. This rapidity is one of syllabic movement, not of tempo; as is seen when a three-syllabled unit occurs in the midst of two-syllabled; there is a triplet; three syllables in the time of two. If the syllabic speed is retarded, the minor stresses tend to become full stresses; that is, the four-syllabled units resolve, each into its two potential two-syllabled units.

A strange transforming effect of the four-syllabled rhythm may here be touched on. Nothing, one would suppose, could be further from its sportiveness than Milton's stately *Hymn on the Nativity*:

It was the wìnter wìld,
While the Hèaven-bòrn chìld
Àll mèanly wràpped in the rùde mànger lìes:
Nàture, in àwe to Hìm,
Had dòffed her gàudy trìm,
With hèr grèat Màster sò to sỳmpathìze:

Alexandrine and heroic alternate, and the whole is undoubtedly in two-syllabled rhythm. This is the metre of many English Canzones, such as Hunt's *O lovely age of gold.* Take a lighter type of verse, however:

A cheer for Robin Hood
And Nottingham's famed wood;
When the greensward was the merry men's resort;
When the tough and springy yew
Was the noblest tree that grew,
And the bow held foremost place in English sport.

(Eliz. Cook, *The Bow*, st. 1.)

If this is read in the same way,

A chèer for Ròbin Hòod
And Nòttinghàm's fàmed wòod;
When the grèensward was the mèrry mèn's resòrt;

it is felt that this is not the reading intended: there is a chafing against the restraint; the movement wishes to speed up, an indication of which is the appearance of the three-syllabled units at the opening of lines

three to six. The stanza is not to be read in the stately
canzone rhythm, but in the sprightlier four-syllabled:

> A chèer for Ròbin Hòod .
>
> And Nòttinghạm's fàmed wòod ;
>
> When the grèensward wạs the mèrry mẹn's resòrt ;

The alternate stresses have become minor stresses,
and the Alexandrine and heroic combination has become a common ballad-verse. This is a notable transformation; but as sea-hearted Proteus was Proteus
whatever bewildering shape he might for the moment
assume, so these two forms, apparently poles apart,
appear to be only different rhythmic manifestations
of one fundamental metre. The actual steps of the
metamorphosis can be seen; an accent dropped here
and there by the substitution of a light for a heavy
syllable; a three-syllabled unit opening a line instead
of a two-syllabled; a less exalted spirit substituted for
one more exalted. Whilst one cannot read the sonorous
canzones of Milton's *Hymn* to the rhythm of the four-
syllabled ballad, yet at the same time one cannot deny
that that vigorous if crepitative rhythm is lying perdu
within those stately measures.

In general, each stress-unit contains one accented
syllable, and one or more unaccented. It may vary,
however, in containing more than one accented syllable, in containing syllables all unaccented, or in
being devoid altogether of syllables. These varying
units must be considered briefly.

The heavy iamb (or spondee), – – (where – is rather
accent than quantity, though it may be both), is com-

mon both in Blank and Lyric. It is found frequently
in the ballads:

> The gòod *whỳte brède*, the gòod *rèd wỳne*,
> And theretò the fỳne *àle bròwn*
>
> (*A Lyttel Geste of Robyn Hode*, fytte 7, st. 40.)

Here the second adjectives have the same accent as
the first adjectives and the nouns, but the adjectives
and nouns riding the wave-crest take the stress, and
thereby receive rhythmical prominence, though the
accents on the three words may be exactly the same
in degree. This is more noticeable when the same word
is repeated:

> Ùp then crèw the rèd *rèd còck*
>
> (*Wife of Usher's Well*, st. 8.)

The first 'red,' which bears stress, is uttered no more
forcibly than the second 'red,' yet it is felt that it has
a quality that the second lacks; the waves of the
temporal metre, pulsing within the hearer or reader,
give prominence to the words that ride the crests; the
prominence may be, and is, of the slightest, but it is
undoubtedly present. However slight, it is sufficient
to point the metre for the hearer; it is so slight that
many, not keenly alive to metre, do not notice it at
all, and cannot hear any difference between verse and
prose, especially between blank verse and prose.

The light iamb (or pyrrhic) ∪ ∪ occurs much more
often in Blank Verse than in Lyric:

> Frìghted the rèign of Chàŏs *ănd òld Nǐght*.

In lyric this would have been avoided in one of two
ways. Either the last unit would have been made one
of one syllable preceded by one of three syllables:

> The reìgn of Chàos *and òld   Nìght*

when it is similar to

> And fìrst he hàrpit a gràve   tùne;

or the words would have been transposed:

> The reìgn of Chàos òld and Nìght.

The unit occurs in a line quoted by Ruskin:

> Shall any following spring revive
> The àsh*ĕs òf* the ùrn?

He writes of how he insisted, "partly in childish ob-
stinacy, and partly in true instinct for rhythm...on
reciting it with an accented *of*...."

Lyric is more generally read than Blank, and by a
section of the people more influenced by decided
rhythm than are those who delight in Blank; and it
is possibly because of an insistence to accent words
that fall on the wave-crest that poets have tended to
keep unemphatic or unaccented words from that
position.

In the following the rhythm is different from that of
the heavy iamb:

> And fìrst he hàrp*it a gràve*   tùne
> And syne he has harpit a gay;
> > *(Glasgerton*, st. 7.)
> She's tà'en a càke *o the bèst*   brèad,
> A stòup *o the bèst*   wìne.
> > *(Fair Annie*, st. 13.)
> O gìve me a shìve *o your brèad,*   lòve,
> O give me a cup o your wine!
> > (*The jolly Goshawk*, st. 32.)

THE STRESS-UNIT

Here it might be supposed that the last unit of the first line was a heavy iamb, preceded by a light iamb

And fìrst he hàrpit a gràve tùne

where the 'a' is made to ride the wave-crest, but without accent, and the 'grave' is advanced to the trough of the wave but retains its accent. In reading this line there would be no hover on 'grave,' the effect being as though 'two' were substituted for 'a':

And fìrst he hàrpit twò gràve tùnes

when the rhythm is similar to

And ùp then crèw the rèd rèd còck.

Retaining the 'a' however, there is a hover on 'grave,' so that a syllable could be inserted between the two words without disturbing the time-value of the unit:

And fìrst he hàrpit a gràver tùne.

It means that there is a three-syllabled unit followed by a unit composed of a hover or pause and one accented syllable.

This one-syllabled unit remains the same, too, when the preceding unit has but two syllables:

The fìrst stèp the làdy stèpped,
She stèpped òn a stòne

(*Lamkin*, st. 18.)

O whà's blùde is thìs, he sàys,
That lieth in my ha'?

(*Ib.* st. 26.)

The first units could be made parallel to the 'red red cock' units by adding 'short'—'the first short step,' and the one in the line following could be made ordinary by making 'stepped' two-syllabled.

The same rhythm may appear in two consecutive units:

> Give me leave to set my horn to my mouth
> And to blòw   blàsts   thrèe.
>
> (*Robin Hood and the curtall Fryer*, 1, 100.)

> It's up, it's up the Couden bank,
> It's down the Couden brae;
> And aye they made the trumpet sound,
> It's à   fàir   plày.
>
> (*Katherine Janfarie*, st. 15.)

> No, there's nothing half so sweet in life
> As lòve's   yòung   drèam.
>
> (Moore, *Love's Young Dream*.)

The rhythm has always no doubt been intentional, though it could arise through syntactical change:

> Or gỳve me *wòundes* dèep and wỳde,
>
> (*A Lyttel Geste of Robyn Hode*, 5, st. 25.)
>
> And thèy besèt the knỳght's castèll
> The *wàlles* àll abòut.
>
> (*Ib.* 6, st. 2.)
>
> Upon àll the *lòndes* thàt I hàve,
> As Ì am a *trèwe* knỳght.
>
> (*Ib.* 6, st. 4.)

It is evident that upon the italicized words becoming one-syllabled, the unit following would lose a syllable and be a parallel of those discussed.

They produce a characteristic effect when opening Alexandrine verses, as in Lord Bowen's *Shadow Land*:

> Hère   grèat   sòuls   in a plènitùde of vìsion,
> Plànned   hìgh   dèeds   as immòrtal as the sùn;

The unit containing one unaccented syllable followed
by a pause is extremely common. It is the normal ending of the first line of Nibelungen verse:

> The lòve that Ì hae chòsen
> I'll thèrewith bè contènt.

The passing of the fourth wave can be felt, and it
may be made audible by the insertion of 'me':

> The lòve that Ì hae chòsen (mè)
> I'll thèrewith bè contènt.

It may occur within the line, as in Burns's

> I hànker,   and cànker,
> To sèe their cùrsed prìde.

The syllable makes what has been earlier in the chapter called a feminine iamb. It is of very common occurrence, and may be thought an objection to considering
the stress the last element of the unit. The objection,
however, is less than it seems. There must often be
sound preceding the stress, or succeeding, whether it
be considered the first element or the last. Prosodists
see no objection to consonantal sound following the
accented vowel, so that 'abreast' is unobjectionable as
an iamb, though the consonantal sound following the
vowel is at least as much as that which goes before.
Again, 'the breasts' would also be accepted as an iamb,
though now the consonantal sound following the accent
is considerably more than that preceding. The words 'the
beater,' however, would not be considered as an iamb,
though the part following the accent takes less time in
enunciation than the part following the accented vowel
in 'the breasts.' In the present marking of the units, it

is immaterial if there is an after-sound, be that sound
a slow broken sibilation or a smooth easy-closing liquid.
Where the closing consonants enter another unit, they
naturally take part of its time, making, as has been
seen, a rippling triple unit.

It is probably because there is so often a syntactical
break following the feminine iamb that its last syllable
has been called extra-metrical, especially in the blank
verse:

Yet hère, Laèr*tes* ! *Abòard*, abòard, for shàme !
(Hamlet, 1, 3, 55.)

Been thùs encòun*ter'd. A fìgure* lìke your father
(Ib. 1, 2, 199.)

If it be objected that the break could hardly occur in
the midst of a unit, and that the unit is normal if the
feminine syllable be rejected,—the objection is met by
units such as the following:

Thus àn*swered. Lèad*er of those àrmies brìght
(P. L., 1 272.)

Tormènt*s him. Ròund* he thròws his bàleful èyes
(Ib. 1, 56.)

Agàinst the ùse of nà*ture? Près*ent fèars
(Macbeth, 1, 3, 137.)

The same construction occurs, too, when the feminine
ending is not present:

Wèll, lèt's awày and sày how mùch is dòne.
(Ib. 3, 3, 22.)

Ò, yèt I dò repènt me of my fùry,
(Ib. 2, 3, 112.)

Again, the feminine may be a double feminine:

Beàtitùde past ùt*terance*; *òn* his rìght
(P. L., 3, 62.)

He gòes forth gàl*lantly. That hè* and Càesar mìght
(Ant. and C., 4, 4, 36.)

The conclusion must be that a unit may quite well be divided by a hover without suffering disintegration. There is, as it were, a slight poise in the midst of the unit; indeed, hovers and poises may be made in any part without destruction of the metre, and being so made they add infinitely to the variety of the rhythm. Moreover, the breaks are syntactical; the under-flowing pulsing metre carries the thought on its wave across the breaches.

As there are heavy two-syllabled units, so there may be heavy three-syllabled units:

Shòw *you swèet Càe*sar's wòunds, pòor pòor dùmb mòuths

(*Jul. Caes.*, 3, 2, 229.)

Your spìr*its shìne thròugh* you. Withìn this hòur at mòst

(*Macbeth*, 3, 1, 128.)

*Like yòung lòv*ers whom yòuth and lòve make dèar

(Shelley, *The Sensitive Plant*, 1, 68.)

To ròof *the glòw-wòrm* from the èvening dèw

(*Ib.* 1, 57.)

Brought plèasure thère *and lèft pàs*sion behìnd

(*Ib.* 2, 24.)

The amount of accent on the second syllable of these three-syllabled units will vary with different readers, some may disregard the accent altogether. In the first two quotations from Shelley, however, there is no doubt that the heavy three-syllabled unit differs from the lighter one that follows it: all that is desired here is to shew that there may be three-syllabled units with two accented syllables, the second one being more prominent through combining accent and stress.

A construction appears in blank verse, which, whilst apparently similar, is of quite a different nature:

A mind not to be chang'd by place or time

(*P. L.* 1, 253.)

For one *restraint, lords of the world* besides

(*Ib.* 1, 32.)

Illumine, what *is low raise and support,*

(*Ib.* 1, 23.)

These three are parallel in construction with the three from Shelley:

Like yòung lòvers whom yòuth and lòve make dèar

A mìnd nòt to be chàng'd by plàce or tìme.

Both contain ten syllables; both contain five accents; the accents are in the same positions in both; yet one is a line of four, the other a verse of five beats.

As has been seen, Shelley's opens with a unit of three syllables; did Milton's open in the same way:

A mìnd nòt to be chàng'd by plàce or tìme,

it would be a line of four beats also. Being intended for Blank Verse, however, it is not read in this way: there is a hover on 'mind,' there is none on 'young':

A mīnd nòt to be chàng'd by plàce or tìme.

That is, the three-syllabled unit is by the hover converted to two units, the first an ordinary iamb composed of two syllables, the second an iamb, composed of hover and syllable. Were the hover made on 'young,' Shelley's lyric line would be changed to Blank Verse:

Like yòung lòvers whom yòuth and lòve make dèar.

Using the conventional signs for short and long, or non-hover and hover, in the lyric line the unit is "lĭke yŏung lŏvers," the Blank Verse units are "lĭke yōung lŏvers."

This heavy three-syllabled unit is, in fact, another of the channels for the transformation of Lyric to Blank, or Blank to Lyric.

It is admitted that the blank verses quoted may be read in another way:

A mìnd nòt to be chàng'd by tìme or plàce

where there is no hover on 'mind,' and the place of the stress is shifted from 'not' to 'to,' but it will be found that this comes very near to the lyric reading. The object of analysis, however, is not to discover what different readings there may be, but in what way the different readings follow one underlying principle: the principle is constant, the application varies with mood and person.

Summarizing the foregoing chapter, the stress-unit is the time interval between two wave-crests of metre. Metre is itself inaudible, and its presence is manifested by sound floating upon its pulsations. Such sound may be inarticulate; may be a mere murmur; or it may be articulate and not understood, yet it may still be metrical. The hearer can say if matter spoken in a foreign tongue is verse or prose. Poetry is emotional speech floating upon a regular metre of varying rhythms: tangible syllabic utterance floating upon intangible metrical waves or pulsations. The natural accents of speech coinciding with the pulsations of the metre, give the stresses, or beats. These stresses are separated by approximately equal periods of time, and the time-period from stress to stress constitutes the stress-unit. The variation in units is primarily in their syllabic burden; secondarily in the almost impalpable expansion and contraction in the time-value of the units,—the *ad lib.* of metre, which is implied when it is said that the time-value of the units is approximately equal. A unit may be altogether silent, or it may contain from one to six syllables; the number is not fixed, nor arbitrary, except that in lyric verse, if the unit contain more than three syllables, the syllables are divided up between a main stress and a minor stress. The unit, which is taken as ending with the stress and beginning immediately after the preceding stress, may have that stress suppressed through having an unaccented syllable coinciding with its incidence, or it may have an accented syllable preceding it in addition to the accented syllable coinciding with the stress. The syllables in a unit may be sequent, or may be divided by a pause, but if so divided they are usually connected by a hover of sound.

So often have the words 'accent' and 'stress' been used that it may seem undue prominence has been given to accent and stress. They are, however, far from being considered prominent. The merest indication of accent here and there is all that is necessary; indeed, once the underflowing temporal metre is felt, nothing more is necessary than ordinary speech-accent. If a stanza be repeated in thought only, it will be found that the stresses may be made as prominent as in speech; that in thought they may appear prominent when they do not exist at all in the speech,—that is, when all syllables, unaccented, accented, or stressed, are spoken with exactly the same force. In fact, the pulsation of the metre is mental, and must be induced before the hearer hears the spoken words as verse. It is the regular fall of the accents in the opening units of a verse that sets the mental pulsations in motion; if those accents give false direction, a false metre pulsates, a jar occurring when this is realized by the hearer. The

child starts with sing-song; as feeling matures the inaudible temporal definiteness of the sing-song remains,
though the speech is moderated to an even and uniform
flow of language. This is the reason that to many people
verse is indistinguishable from prose: they fail to feel
the underflowing metre. When, too, they dispute regarding the scansion say of the first verse of *Paradise
Lost*, the dispute is usually about the syntactical
arrangement of the words. So long, however, as it is
recognized that Blank Verse for instance consists of
five comparatively equal temporal units, upon which
the rhythm of the words may float in many varying
forms, ground for disagreement disappears. The rhythm
may vary according to individual fancy; the underflowing metre must be the same for all. The metre is
felt even in French poetry, which obeys its laws, even
though that poetry has no accents.

It may be convenient to give a table of the units
that form rhythmical schemes:

     1. Iamb ∪ ⸝

     2. Anapaest ∪ ∪ ⸝

     3. Diiamb ∪ ˘ ∪ ⸝

1. The iamb varies from pyrrhic ∪ ∪ to spondee ⸝ ⸝
and the feminine iamb ∪ ⸝ ∪ (amphibrach) gives rise to
the trochee ⸝ ∪, which seems sometimes to form a
rhythmical scheme: it varies from ˘ ∪ to ⸝ −. Neither
variation of iamb or trochee, nor the feminine iamb, forms
rhythmical schemes. The dactyl ⸝ ∪ ∪ springs from the
double feminine iamb ∪ ⸝ ∪ ∪.

2. The anapaest varies from $\smile\smile\acute{\smile}$ to $\smile\underset{|}{\acute{-}}\acute{-}$, and springs directly from the iamb. When it drops a syllable it can hardly be said to vary, as it simply returns to the parent form.

3. The diiamb (a name used here for convenience) varies from $\smile\underset{|}{\curlyvee}\smile\acute{-}$ to $\smile\underset{|}{\acute{\curlyvee}}\smile\acute{-}$, and the rhythmical scheme is a blending of these two, syllables being freely dropped on either side of the minor stress. The dropping of syllables does not make this rhythm three-syllabled or two-syllabled. The four-syllabled unit of Blank Verse, $\smile\smile\smile\underset{|}{\acute{-}}$, never comes near making a rhythmical scheme; it is used only as a rare variant, altogether different in character from the diiamb. The same is true of the five-syllabled unit, $\smile\smile\smile\smile\underset{|}{\acute{-}}$.

Practically all rhythmical schemes are a mingling of various units; it can only be said of the above three that schemes may be formed where they predominate. It is useless, too, to attempt to assign definite values to the signs $\smile$ and $-$; they continually vary; their values may differ in adjacent units, may continually fluctuate; but their aggregate in one unit approximately equals their aggregate in another. It is useless, too, to attempt a list of all the possible units that may be used as variations; the number is infinite.

Is there any observable physical basis for stress-units? Remembering that poetry and music have evolved together and have many characteristics in common, it will be conceded that any natural function influencing the one is likely to have influenced the other.

In music, the semibreve is called the mother of all

the notes. In ancient music it had two values; in imperfect time, or lesser prolation, its value was a bar of present common time; in perfect time, or greater prolation, a bar and a half. In singing it was indicated by a down-beat, and an up-beat, these two beats being represented by two minims. There was a definite value for these two minims; they were of the same duration as the beat of the human pulse. In a psalm-book of 1688, on the other hand, a breve is said to be "about the duration of eight pulses at the wrist of a person in good health and temper." This would make two pulses to the minim. It may be that one deals with the heart-beat, the other with the pulse; but in either case, the heart-beat is the function controlling the length of the note. The beat of the heart is divided into two unequal parts; a third or a fourth of the time of duration of the beat is occupied by the systole of the auricles; a fourth by the state of quiescence, and half or nearly half by the systole of the ventricles. Laennec, who makes this approximation, continues, "Each beat of the arterial pulse corresponds to this double sound, in other words, to two sounds. One of them is clear and rapid...The other is more dull and prolonged..." The pulsation may, in fact, be represented by the signs ◡ – (short, long); and, as in listening to the ticking of a clock an accent can be imagined first on one tick, then on the other, so an accent can be imagined, first on the ◡, then on the –; if on the ◡ the effect is that of the trochee, ◡́ –; if on the –, the effect is that of the iamb, ◡ –́.

Normally, the heart makes an average of 72 pulsations in a minute. Ruskin reckoned two paces in walking the average taken in a second, concluding from this that the proper length of the spondee was one second; and on this basis he reckoned the temporal values of the classic feet, which might, under varying conditions, be quickened or delayed. Thus he took the pace instead of the heart-beat as the primary physical basis of metre. The pace itself, however, appears to have a connection with the heart-beat, for in ordinary marching to the sounds of music 75 steps a minute are taken,—almost the average of the heart-pulsations in a minute. Ruskin's average pace is too fast;—two in a second, 120 in a minute, is the speed of the 'storming march,' the 'quick march' being 108.

Ordinary speech varies from about 60 to 180 words a minute, say an average of 120 words, or 160 to 170 syllables. Lanier considers 180 a slow rate of utterance, and experiment seems to shew him to be correct.

It is difficult to judge if the number of syllables spoken is in such agreement with the heart-beat as the notes of music apparently were. Singing must have been slow and deliberate, for the church minim appears to have approximately, if not actually, the same value as the secular crotchet.

In reading aloud, too, or in reciting, when the emotional element in the verses increases, there is an inclination to read or recite faster; and increase of emotion increases the speed of the heart-beat. The speed at which different individuals read the same poem varies. There appears to be some connection, but it baffles definition; it may be subtle, it is more likely to be simple; but whatever it is, it is there.

Remembering too, how often the trochaic rhythm is ◡ –, and the iambic ◡ –, some reason may be conjectured for the tilt from trochaic to iambic that has taken place in the predominant rhythm of British verse. As any observer may note from personal experience, in times of high emotion the short beat of the heart is the more prominent; the pulsation is decidedly ◡ –. As emotion calms down, so the short beat becomes less and less prominent until, when emotion is quiescent, the accent seems transferred to the long beat ◡ –. The change, in fact, is from trochaic to iambic. So the change in the character of the people themselves has been from more elemental passion to one of calmer emotion. With the change in the position of the accent, too, the position of the rime changed, head-rime, or alliteration, becoming end-rime.

CHAPTER III

THE VERSE-UNIT

NEXT to the stress-unit, the smallest uniform aggregate of parts is the verse. This in lyric normally contains eight stress-units or their temporal equivalent, and when printed, is usually divided for convenience, into two equal parts. Each part of a verse so divided, or divided into smaller parts, is commonly known as a line.

From a casual examination of printed poetry, the length of a line, that is, the number of its stress-units, would appear to be quite arbitrary. It would appear that it rests with the poet himself to decide whether a line shall contain one stress-unit only, or include the whole verse. Whilst the length of the line is thus under his complete control, it is otherwise with the verse.

The length of the line may range from one two-syllabled unit, as in Herrick:

> Thus I
> Pass by
> And die:
> As one
> Unknown,
> And gone:

to eight three-syllabled units, as in Tennyson:

Fame blowing out from her golden trumpet a jubilant challenge
    to Time and to Fate;

The poet is at perfect liberty to print the verse as he pleases; so that Coleridge's verse will by one poet be printed:

> The fair breeze blew, the white foam flew,
>   The furrow followed free;

whilst by another it will be printed:

> The fair breeze blew,
> The white foam flew,
> The furrow followed free;

It is to be observed, however, that the verse had assumed definiteness before the poet could have had any thought of printing at all; it assumed definiteness whilst still recited or sung only, and before committed to writing in any way. So absolute was this definiteness that on the introduction of printing it required no ingenuity to set out the verses in a way that has not to this day changed in any essential particular. If it be objected that the printer had manuscript to guide him, the remark need but be transferred to the writer of the manuscripts, and he had no guide but his ear. In many instances, too, the verses in manuscript were run on without punctuation or division of any kind; as though the writer, having the divisions in his mind, assumed that the reader would have them in his mind likewise and needed no guide. Others, whose ears were less certain, assumed a like uncertainty in the reader, and marked the divisions with colons, or periods, or some equivalent device. The point is, that it was always possible to make the divisions, even when they were not indicated in the script.

There must, of course, have been many irregular verses existing side by side with the norm of eight units; but once the norm was perceived, unconsciously or otherwise, the irregular verses became fewer, being either modified, or dropped.

In the collection of old Danish ballads by Grundtvig, many such irregular verses have been preserved; more would have been preserved in Percy's collection, if Percy had not seen fit to restore those he considered defective. Fortunately, an old version of the ballad of *Chevy Chase* has been preserved, and a comparison of this with Percy's version shews in a most instructive way how Percy played the part of Procrustes.

The verse of eight stress-units is the norm in the old Romances, and has therefore been called the Romance metre. From it have risen three characteristic variants, and each of the three seems to have been particularly adopted by the three European nations that appear to have most in common; the Alexandrine by France, the Nibelungen by Germany, the Ballad by England. The three variants appear in common in all the countries, as in all countries whose poetry has become accentual; but the Alexandrine, first extensively used in France in the epic of Alexander, has become the vehicle for French drama; in the Nibelungen metre was written the great German epic of the Nibelungen Noth; and in the Ballad metre is written the great bulk of English popular poetry.

The Romance verse and the three variants are shewn below:

```
Romance:      ∪ ⏤ ∪ ⏤ ∪ ⏤ ∪ ⌢   ∪ ⏤ ∪ ⏤ ∪ ⏤ ∪ ⏤ ⌢
              |   |   |   |         |   |   |   |
Alexandrine:  ∪ ⏤ ∪ ⏤ ∪ ⏤       ∪ ⏤ ∪ ⏤ ∪ ⏤
              |   |   |   |         |   |   |   |
Nibelungen:   ∪ ⏤ ∪ ⏤ ∪ ⏤ ∪     ∪ ⏤ ∪ ⏤ ∪ ⏤
              |   |   |   |         |   |   |   |
Ballad:       ∪ ⏤ ∪ ⏤ ∪ ⏤ ∪ ⏤   ∪ ⏤ ∪ ⏤ ∪ ⏤
              |   |   |   |         |   |   |   |
```

The three variants have one feature in common; all have dropped the last unit of the verse. The Alexandrine

has in addition dropped the last unit of the first half
of the verse; the Nibelungen has dropped only the last
syllable of that unit. In every instance where a unit or
part of a unit has been dropped, its place is taken by
a sonant hover, and the syllable dropped may at any
time be restored, when the hover disappears so far as
it occupied the place of syllables.

All three variations form distinct and distinctive
rhythmic schemes, or they can be mingled at will,
with one another and with the full romance verse.
Their identity is at once apparent when they appear
together:

Mỳ Pèggy smìleṣ sae swèetly, whenè'er we mèet alàne,
I wìsh nae maìr to lày my càre, I wìsh nae màir of à' that's ràre,

By whòm was Dàvid tàught to àim the dèadly blòw...
No swòrd nor spèar the strìpling tòok but chòse a pèbble of the
    bròok.

In the first a full Romance verse follows a Nibelungen
verse, in the second it follows an Alexandrine; and the
hovers at the places where syllables have been dropped
are unmistakable, the passing of the wave-crest being
clearly felt. The contrast of Alexandrine and Ballad
alternating has always proved attractive in English
ears; the resulting rhythm has been given a particular
name, Poulter's measure.

In còurt whosò demàundes   what dàme doth mòst
    excèl,
For mỳ concèit I mùst neèds sày, Faìr Brìdges bèars
    the bèll

Here the final Romance verse has been shortened to
a Ballad verse; and that there is a pause at the end
of the Ballad verse equivalent to the unit dropped is
made evident by the readiness with which the dropped
syllables, when restored, enter into and complete the
rhythm:

> We played at love in Mulga town,
>   And O her eyes were blue!
> We played at love in Mulga town,
>   And love's a game for two.
> If three should play, alack-a-day!
>   There's one of them will rue,
>   *Dear Heart!*
> There's one of them will rue.
>   (Ogilvie, *In Mulga Town*, st. 1.)

This stanza would round off quite naturally at the
first 'rue,' when it would end with a Ballad verse.
That the pause following all the odd short lines is
temporally equal to a stress-unit is shewn by the
addition of the two syllables 'Dear Heart.' These,
comprising a stress-unit, make the second half of the
Ballad verse equal to half of a Romance verse: the
imagination immediately recognizes this, and knowing
from the earlier part of the stanza that the scheme is
Ballad, a Ballad conclusion is expected, and comes
with the repetition of the sixth line:

> If three should play, alack-a-day!
> There's one of them will rue, Dear Heart!
>   There's one of them will rue.

There is here as it were a telescoping of an eight-
stressed verse with a seven-stressed, the former resulting when the first two lines are taken together, the
latter when the last two are taken; the second line, in
fact, is common to both.

The special point to be observed is that the pause following the seven-stressed or Ballad verse is of sufficient duration to admit of its place being taken by a stress-unit; and when its place is so taken the pause disappears. The inference is that whenever a verse containing only seven stress-units occurs, the pause by which it is followed is simply a gap from which sound has been dropped, and into which sound may at any time be replaced without altering the temporal value of the verse. The pause may not always, and need not necessarily, be exactly equal temporally to the dropped unit of sound; for a pause being unable to assert itself as articulate sound is able, it has a tendency to collapse on itself as it were, to shorten unequally. Nevertheless, the passing of the wave of the underflowing metre is felt even in the pause, and the more clearly the passing is felt the more definite will the pause be made. It must be iterated that the pause need not mean a cessation of sound, but may be bridged with a sonant hover.

During the time that the full verse of eight stress-units was emerging from amongst verses of an irregular number of units, poetry was commonly sung or recited. Great regard must naturally be given to facility of delivery. In speech, a sentence consists of as much thought as may readily be conveyed in one breath; the more syntactically broken an emotional thought is in its utterance, the less forcible it becomes; and it follows that the most incisively uttered thought is that which can be uttered distinctly in one breath. The most incisive spoken thoughts are those which appeal most directly to the emotions, and a sentence will consequently be shorter or longer as it is more or less emotional.

The earliest poetry was probably almost purely emotional, bare of all ornament of rime, alliteration, metre, or even rhythm; it was simply ejaculatory. The first ornament was metaphor; then came rhythmic expression, then metre, pointed first with alliteration and then rime. Music followed early, coming in probably with rhythmic expression; dance and metre seem to enter together.

Among the Maori people poetry may be studied in many stages of evolution; from irregularly rhythmical laments and love-songs, to regularly rhythmical posture-dances, incantations, game-songs, and war-songs. Many of the war-songs were on the verge of metre and rime, when their development was rudely interrupted and arrested by civilization. Their nearness to metre and rime was shewn by the readiness with which the Maori immediately adopted both, the old and the new living side by side, the Maori understanding and appreciating both, the European only his own.

It would appear that the dance of motion and gesture was the force controlling the rhythm and creating the metre of poetry and its handmaiden music; once the metre was established, it developed independently of the dance. In later times poetry was in a measure divorced from music, and both developed independently.

In rhythmic poetry the sentences are of varying length; in metrical poetry they tend to assume a uniform length, an average of the length of rhythmical or emotional sentences; in other words, the average length of a breath.

This average had long been established when the
Metrical Romances became popular in England, but
the evolution of the verse-form or verse-norm was still
in progress, there as elsewhere. The most characteristic, and the most widely accepted variant of the full
verse of eight units was the variant in which the last
unit is dropped, making a verse of seven units.

Professor Saintsbury thinks this seven-unit verse
"the nearest actual, and almost the nearest possible,
approach to the original Anglo-Saxon line or pair of
hemistichs. The octosyllabic couplet, which was at first
preferred,...differs from this line in the more or less
exact equality of the hemistichs, whereas the Old
English pair rather inclined to shorten the second;
but the fourteener retains this relationship." It could be
wished that examples had been given, but Professor
Saintsbury notes that the statement is made after wide
reading. In view of the reason for the shortening, too,
the tendency towards it is perfectly natural.

During the early days of the Romance metre in
England, the Church, joining issue with Heathenesse
in its own lists of song, wrote "Lives of the Saints" in
the popular measure of the Metrical Romances. This
measure still pervades the Church Hymns, Ancient and
Modern, and these hymns have in a most important
particular faithfully preserved the old metre. They are
distinguished as being chiefly in three "measures";—
L.M. (long measure), C.M. (common measure), and
S.M. (short measure), these being respectively in verses
of sixteen, fourteen, and twelve syllables of two-
syllabled rhythm. In the music of the hymns it will be
found that almost every verse of two lines, whether

L.M., C.M., or S.M.—more, that every verse even of
five stress-units—is sung to sixteen crotchets, or sixteen syllables.

If, again, a congregation be watched whilst singing
any of these hymns, the quick dilation of the breast
due to the taking of breath will be seen taking place
after every line, or four bars.

The choir may or may not have been trained to take
the breath after every eighth bar; the full verse can
easily be sung in one breath.

The same no doubt took place when the minstrel
sang the Metrical Romance; he either took a breath
after each line, or after each verse; and if taken in the
way in which it is taken by most congregations, it was
more in the nature of a gasp than a leisurely breath.

The last unit was dropped in order that there need
be no gasp after the singing of the fourteen syllables.
Either that, or there were two forms developed side by
side, each suiting, perhaps, some particular manner of
delivery; the Romance, where the gasp was tolerated,
and the Ballad, where the breath was taken in the
time-space of the dropped unit. The Anglo-Saxon
verse, shortening in the second half, evidently represents the prototype of the Ballad. This being a natural
development, it will doubtless be found in all accentual
poetry, of whatsoever country.

If the Metrical Romances only were taken into consideration, the verse-unit might be taken as one of four
stress-units. Against this, however, is the undoubted
fact that the Ballad, varying from the full verse, evidently varied for the sake of the breathing space at
the end of the verse. This variation would have been

unnecessary had the breath been taken after every line of four stresses. Even had it varied so that the first breath might be avoided and seven units instead of four be taken in a breath, that would still uphold the contention that the eight-stress verse is the verse-unit. Moreover, in both Romance metre and Ballad metre the full verse encloses the full sentence; and in reciting, the Romance couplet usually, and the Ballad couplet invariably, are uttered in one breath.

It seems unnecessary to quote examples to shew that verse-unit and sentence are coterminous;—the awkwardness resulting when they are not coterminous may be felt on a reading of Browning's *Reverie*.

As the full verse, whether Romance or Ballad, is usually divided into two equal portions, so the sentence contained in them is usually similarly divided into two clauses. As in the course of the arrow shot upwards there are two parts, the ascent and the descent, with a slight hover in the air as the arrow turns, so in the full verse there are two parts, and a slight hover at their union that welds but does not crush them together:

Ye banks and braes o' bonie Doon, ⌢ how can ye bloom sae fresh and fair?
How can ye chant, ye little birds, ⌢ and I sae weary, fu' o' care?

These full verses of Burns's *The Banks o' Doon* are usually printed in lines of four stress-units:

> Ye banks and braes o' bonie Doon,
>> How can ye bloom sae fresh and fair?
> How can ye chant, ye little birds,
>> And I sae weary, fu' o' care?

Burns wrote three sets of this song; the above is the third,—"which, being the worst, is naturally the most popular," said Burns. The first set, *Sweet are the Banks*, is in stanzas of twelve lines; the first eight follow:

> Sweet are the banks, the banks o' Doon,
>   The spreading flowers are fair,
> And everything is blythe and glad,
>   But I am fu' o' care.
> Thou'lt break my heart, thou bonie bird,
>   That sings upon the bough!
> Thou minds me o' the happy days
>   When my fause Luve was true.

The second set, *Ye flowery Banks*, is in stanzas of four lines:

> Ye flowery banks o' bonie Doon,
>   How can ye blume sae fair?
> How can ye chant, ye little birds,
>   And I sae fu' o' care?
>
> Thou'lt break my heart, thou bonie bird,
>   That sings upon the bough:
> Thou minds me o' the happy days
>   When my fause Luve was true!

The three sets are printed to shew, partly the varying from Ballad to Romance, partly how the sentence and full verse are coterminous. Is there any question that the sentences contained in the Ballad verses are said each in a breath? The writer knows from experience that among the Maori people sentences of three and four times the length of Romance verses may be and are commonly taken in one breath.

In the whole range of lyric poetry, the writer has not found a verse exceeding eight stress-units in length. He came on Tennyson's *God and the Universe*:

Will my tiny spark of being wholly vanish in your deeps and
  heights?
Must my day be dark by reason, O ye Heavens, of your
  boundless nights,
Rush of Suns, and roll of systems, and your fiery clash of
  meteorites?

Is not every reader, though conscious of the rhythm of
the verses, conscious also of a certain inharmony in the
metre? The consciousness may be dulled by frequent
reading,—but on a first reading it is certainly present.
If read as follows:

Will my tiny spark of being wholly vanish in your heights?
Must my days be dark by reason, Heavens, of your boundless
  nights,
Rush of Suns, and roll of systems, fiery clash of meteorites?

Has not the sense of inharmony disappeared? In the
second reading, each verse contains eight units; in the
first, each contains nine;—the intruding ninth was the
cause of the inharmony.

The stanza is rather odic in form than lyric; and in
the ode, lyric lines and heroic verses may mingle in
almost heterogeneous manner, for the ode is intended
to be sung;—and as noted regarding the Church hymns,
all verses, of whatever number of units, are there reduced to one metre, the long metre. Tennyson uses
the stanza at an earlier date in the odic form:

> Roman Virgil, thou that singest
>   Ilion's lofty temples robed in fire,
> Ilion falling, Rome arising,
>   wars, and filial faith, and Dido's pyre;
>
> *(To Virgil,* st. 1.)

This does not seem inharmonious, because like the
Canzone it is printed in the odic form, where verses
and lines mingle irregularly: it seems inharmonious

when printed in one long verse because the greatest length of the lyric verse is eight units. Moreover, it will be found that the reading of the odic forms is as a rule statelier and more deliberate than that of the lyric.

Regarding the Nibelungen, it must be noted that in the great repository of this rhythm, the Nibelungen Noth, many stanzas occur with a swell in the fourth verse:

Now came the lovely maiden, as morning steals in rose
Forth from the sullen shadows; then slipped their many woes
From men's faint hearts, new gladdened to have old aches
   dispelled:
He saw the lovely maiden, her grace and her splendour he beheld.

(Adv. 5, st. 17.)

This follows the original in rhythm and syntactical division. The full verse, the fourth, is an unusual type in British poetry, but it appears in Tennyson:

It is the miller's daughter, and she is grown so dear, so dear,
That I would be the jewel that trembles in her ear:
For hid in ringlets day and night, I'd touch her neck so warm
   and white.

Here the first verse is one of these Nibelungen-Romance verses; the second is ordinary Nibelungen; the third is full Romance: the identity of the three is apparent. The verse is also used by Burns in the first four verses of *Sae Flaxen were her Ringlets*:

> Sae flaxen were her ringlets,
>   Her eyebrows of a darker hue,
> Bewitchingly o'er-arching
>   Twa laughing een o' bonie blue.
> Her smiling, sae wiling,
>   Wad make a wretch forget his woe!
> What pleaure, what treasure,
>   Unto those rosy lips to grow!

Such was my Chloris' bonie face
　When first that bonie face I saw,
And ay my Chloris' dearest charm—
　She says she lo'es me best of a' !

(St. 1.)

Here, again, the last two verses swell to full Romance.

Whilst the Alexandrine is clearly divided by a silent unit following the third, a tendency has arisen to vary the form by obliterating the pause, and with it the silent unit. On a first reading of the Earl of Surrey's Psalm 8 there will probably be a stumbling as regards the rhythm:

But yet among all these I ask, "What thing is man?"
Whose turn to serve in his poor need this work Thou first began.
Or what is Adam's son that bears his father's mark?
For whose delight and comfort eke Thou hast wrought all this work.
I see Thou mind'st him much, that does reward him so:
Being but earth, to rule the earth, whereon himself doth go.

Not till the third stanza is reached is it clear that a silent unit divides the verse into two parts;

But yèt amòng all thèse　I àsk what thìng is màn?

This paused Alexandrine is in French called "Alexandrin classique," and all French verse in this rhythm took the classical form until the time of Victor Hugo, when a "vers trimetre" was introduced, which was a verse of six stress-units broken into three equal parts by two hovers, as if the last verse quoted above were:

Being but earth, to rule the earth, where he doth go.

Examples of it may be found in Tennyson's *The First Quarrel*; see verse 1 of stanza 4.

The "vers trimetre," but without hovers, appears in Browning's *Pheidippides*, and in *Fifine at the Fair*. If the following words were met as here printed: "But, when you would dissect the structure, piece by piece, you found, enwreathed amid the country product— fleece and feather, thistle-fluffs and bearded windle-straws"—would there be any doubt of their being prose? Even when printed as verse:

> But, when you would dissect the structure, piece by piece,
> You found, enwreathed amid the country product—fleece
> And feather, thistle-fluffs and bearded windle-straws—
>
> (Section 9, verse 7,)

it is at first difficult to catch the rhythm, as the mid-pause has been obliterated. It appears in the next verse:

> Some shred of foreign silk, unravelling of gauze.

It is then seen that a pause, a silent unit, is intended:

> But, when you would dissect   the structure, piece by piece,
> You found, enwreathed amid   the country product—fleece
> And feather, thistle-fluffs   and bearded windle-straws—
> Some shred of foreign silk,   unravelling of gauze.

It may indeed be that no pause was intended; it may be that readers in whom the temporal metre does not beat strongly will find no need for the pause; will find the verses metrical without it. It is evident, however, that the French "vers trimetre" and the English unpaused Alexandrine are both variants derived from the paused Alexandrine; and as the paused Alexandrine mingles with five-stressed verse, so the unpaused Alexandrine mingles with lyric, as in Shelley's *Skylark*:

> Hail to thee, blithe spirit!
> Bird thou never wert,
> That from heaven or near it,
> Pourest thy full heart
> In profuse strains of unpremeditated art.

In most of the stanzas of this poem, however, the closing Alexandrine is paused:

What love of thine own kind? what ignorance of pain?

but few readers would make more than the slightest hover on the "un" of "unpremeditated" and most would read it without any hover at all. At the same time, it is probable that any reader with intense feeling for metre, will unconsciously feel it to be the equivalent of a paused Alexandrine.

The basic verse-units of lyric poetry then are:

1. Romance.
2. Ballad.
3. Nibelungen, with variant Nibelungen-Romance.
4. Alexandrine, with variant Alexandrine trimetre and Unpaused Alexandrine.

These are shewn with units marked:

1. Ye bànks and bràes o' bònie Dòon, how càn ye blòom sae frèsh and fàir?

2. There blèw a dròwsy dròwsy wìnd, dèep slèep upòn me fèll,

3. From Grèenland's ìcy mountàins, from India's còral strànd,
   It ìs the mìller's dàughter, and shè is gròwn so dèar, so dèar,

4. What lòve of thìne own kìnd? what ìgnorànce of pàin?
   In pròfuse stràins of ùnpremèditàted àrt.
   or
   In pròfuse stràins of ùn- premèditàted àrt.

In looking over any volume of poetry, the reader will soon see that there are certain combinations of lines that do not come under any of the above verse-units.

In the old ballad of *Sir Cauline* there are, as Percy
noted, several irregular stanzas:—stanzas, that is, of
more than two verses of four lines:

> Fair Christabelle, that lady bright,
>   Was had forth of the towre;
> But ever she droopeth in her mynde,
> As nipt by an ungentle winde
>   Doth some faire lillye flowre.

In the second half of the stanza the same thing has
happened that happened in the stanza of *Mulga Town*,
quoted earlier; a Romance verse and a Ballad verse
have been combined, the middle line being made common to both.

What then has happened to the breath-unit? It will
be remembered that the breath-unit or verse-unit that
evolved was the average unit that could be spoken in
one breath; that implies that there were units greater
and smaller, and many of these have become fixed as
definite variations. It will be found that in reading a
ballad aloud, every full verse is invariably taken in a
breath; it will also be found that when an amplified verse
such as the above occurs, that unit is likewise taken in a
breath; in fact, the average unit is an easy average. The
three lines could easily have been reduced to two, but it
was felt that there was no need for such reduction.

Ruskin considered the verse:

> Shout round me, let me hear thee shout, thou happy
>   shepherd-boy!

the longest verse admitted, or possible to the breath.
To a good singer or speaker such a verse is a trifle;
it is not impossible to sing in one breath a phrase
taking from fifteen to twenty seconds.

As noted, the breve is said to be "about the duration of eight pulses at the wrist of a person in good
health and temper." The very name of this note, breve,
is an indication that there was a yet longer note. This
longer note was twice the length of a breve in imperfect time, three times its value in perfect time. It was
called the longa, or long, and represented sixteen pulse-
beats; and in view of what has been said regarding the
controlling influence of the heart, the condition requiring
the person to be "in good health and temper" was no
mere facetiousness.

Church music has departed from the old values of
its notes, so that now the minim of Church music and
the crotchet of secular music are of approximately
equal value, if they are not actually equal. The breve
is now used as a note of indefinite value, occurring in
places where a varied number of syllables are to be
sung to one note, as in the unmetrical Psalms.

The average verse of eight units varies by contract-
ing as well as by amplifying, or rather there must be
lesser as well as greater units to make the average.
Two units may be dropped from one or both
verses:

> The chord, the harp's full chord is hushed,
>   The voice hath died away,
> Whence music, like sweet waters, gushed
>   But yesterday.
>
> (Hemans, *Music of Yesterday*, st. 1.)

> Thou borrowest from that heaven of blue,
>   Oh! maiden dear!
> The depth of that cerulean hue
>   In which thine eyes appear.
>
> (C. Mackay, *Ninette*, st. 1.)

Pleasure! why thus desert the heart
  In its spring-tide?
I could have seen her, I could part
  And but have sigh'd!

O'er every youthful charm to stray,
  To gaze, to touch,—
Pleasure! why take so much away,
  Or give so much?

(Landor, No. 4 of Selections.)

Swinburne was evidently taken with the Landor model, for he used it in his poem *In memory of Walter Savage Landor*, and in *Faustine*. He shortened the fourth line still further in his *Adieux à Marie Stuart*:

Queen, for whose house my fathers fought,
  With hopes that rose and fell,
Red star of boyhood's fiery thought,
  Farewell.

(St. 1.)

In Romance metre the shortening of the fourth line results in the stanza of the favourite *La Belle Dame*:

I set her on my pacing steed,
  And nothing else saw all day long;
For sideways would she lean, and sing
  A faery's song.

(Keats, La Belle Dame sans Merci, st. 5.)

Other variants of the verse will be considered in Chapter V, 'On the Stanza-unit.'

CHAPTER IV

THE HEROIC COUPLET AND BLANK VERSE

THE lyric measures hitherto discussed exclude Blank
Verse, and all measures in Heroic Couplets; all
poetry, that is, whose measure is a verse of *five* stress-
units. The verses of lyric poetry always contain an
even number of stress-units; eight in Romance metre,
all audible; eight in Ballad and Nibelungen, seven
audible, and one represented by the verse-end breath-
pause; and eight in Alexandrine, six audible, and
two represented by pauses, one at the mid-verse and
one at the verse-end. It might be supposed that Heroic
and Blank Verse should likewise be composed of an
even number of stress-units, five audible, and one
represented by the verse-end pause; but, whilst the
pause is always present in a degree more or less pronounced, and whilst it is apparently filled at times,
making an Alexandrine, it is not a breath-pause in the
sense that the verse-end pause in Lyric is a breath-
pause. Moreover, the Alexandrine resulting from the
apparent filling is not an unpaused Alexandrine, but
one broken by a mid-pause, a verse which has been
shewn to contain eight units. It is evident, too, that
the Heroic is in the nature of an intermediary form
only; a form distinctly end-stopped by rime, but a
form whose natural tendency in a certain direction
is so powerful that the evolving overflow from verse
to verse is unhindered, except temporarily, by the
dam of rime, which it immerses, weakens, and almost

obscures; and finally, in the highest blank verse, entirely sweeps away and obliterates.

A fundamental difference between Lyric and Blank Verse is that the lyric measures break up into individual verses of eight stress-units. Each verse contains a complete thought-sentence, and splits again into two equal parts, each containing a complete clause of the thought-sentence; these halves may again subdivide, and on each subdivision of the rhythm the included sentence likewise subdivides into its natural sub-clauses, so that the thought and rhythm swing and sway together, the double rhythm being accentuated by rime at the main division, and often at the minor divisions also, the verse becoming a flashing rime-facetted jewel of thought. Blank Verse, on the other hand, culminating through the Heroic—or of which the Heroic may perhaps be called an elaborated by-product—is a coherent mass, breaking up into irregular portions consisting of a number, small or great, of verses and parts of verses, welded together by the unrestrained flow of thought from verse to verse. Each verse by no means necessarily contains a complete thought-sentence, nor does every sentence necessarily occupy a whole verse. When broken, the verses are broken irregularly, and the rime-facets are altogether absent.

The two measures, Lyric and Blank, have seemingly evolved for the purpose of fulfilling two different func-tions in poetic utterance; the Lyric for song, the Blank for declamation. Hence at the one extreme we have the plebeian Lyrics of the ballad-makers, and at the other the aristocratic Blanks of Milton; and whilst in

the genus of the Lyric those caged in rime are the
sweetest singers, the spirit of the Heroic was of wider
flight and ever beat against the bars of rime, until in
the Blank it found unrimed and unconfined spacious-
ness of utterance in the imagination of the epic, and
the emotion of the drama.

So powerful was the influence of the earlier Lyric,
that the Blank first appeared with rime—in the Heroic
couplet, a ten-syllabled verse that seemed to take the
earlier eight-syllabled line as model.

The first considerable body of verse in Heroic Couplets was Chaucer's *Canterbury Tales*. The form was
adopted and refined by later and lesser poets, and with
their works as models, rules were devised governing the
construction of the verses. It was held that every verse
must contain five accents, and every accent must govern
a foot, in this treatise called unit, of two syllables, so
that the full verse should contain ten syllables. Every
verse should have a caesura, or pause, after the fourth,
fifth, or sixth syllable. There were two forms of the
Heroic that developed side by side; the end-stopped,
and the run-on or enjambed. In the former the sentence and the verse, or the clause and the verse, should
be coterminous, and the thought should be complete
at least in the couplet, if not in the verse. In this the
influence of the Lyric is seen; and the rimes of the
couplet gave definiteness, as in the Lyric, to the verse-
ends and the thought-ends. In the run-on form of the
Heroic, however, the thought need not be confined to
a verse or even to a couplet; in fact, the object aimed
at was to run one verse into another; to allow the
thought to overflow, so that the definiteness of the
couplet was lost. This form, in which the rime loses its

chief function, seems to reveal the purpose, apparently, for which the ten-syllabled verse evolved; that is, the production of a form different in measure from Lyric, in which the thoughts need not be confined each to a verse of definite length, but might contract or dilate according to the emotion to be expressed at the moment. This will be more evident when examples from Blank Verse are examined. Pope and Dryden are two of the chief writers of the Heroic Couplet; the following, shewing the end-stopped couplet, is from Pope's *Essay on Criticism*:

> But most by numbers judge a poet's song ;
> And smooth or rough, with them, is right or wrong ;
> In the bright Muse, though thousand charms conspire,
> Her voice is all these tuneful fools admire ;
> Who haunt Parnassus but to please their ear,
> Not mend their minds ; as some to Church repair,
> Not for the doctrine, but the music there.
> These equal syllables alone require,
> Tho' oft the ear the open vowels tire ;
> While expletives their feeble aid do join ;
> And ten low words oft creep in one dull line :
> While they ring round the same unvary'd chimes,
> With sure return of still expected rhymes ;
> Where e'er you find "the cooling western breeze,"
> In the next line, it "whispers through the trees" :
> If crystal streams "with pleasing murmurs creep,"
> The reader's threaten'd (not in vain) with "sleep" :
> Then, at the last and only couplet fraught
> With some unmeaning thing they call a thought,
> A needless Alexandrine ends the song
> That, like a wounded snake, drags its slow length along.
> Leave such to tune their own dull rhymes, and know
> What's roundly smooth, or languishingly slow ;
> And praise the easy vigour of a line,
> Where Denham's strength, and Waller's sweetness join.

True ease in writing comes from art, not chance,
As those move easiest who have learn'd to dance.
'Tis not enough no harshness gives offence,
The sound must seem an Echo to the sense:
Soft is the strain when Zephyr gently blows,
And the smooth stream in smoother numbers flows;
But when loud surges lash the sounding shore,
The hoarse, rough verse should like the torrent roar:
When Ajax strives some rock's vast weight to throw,
The line too labours, and the words move slow;
Not so, when swift Camilla scours the plain,
Flies o'er th' unbending corn, and skims along the main.

(Verses 337–373.)

The extract itself forms an excellent commentary on the end-stopped couplet, containing as it does Pope's precepts for its construction. It will be observed that on the whole the rules given above are adhered to fairly closely. Most of the verses have the regular five accents, and the required ten syllables, as in:

And smòoth or ròugh, with thèm, is rìght or wròng;

In some of the verses, however, such as:

The sòund must sèem an Ècho to the sènse:

there are but four accents, marked with the sign ` above the words, though the five stress-units, marked with the sign ₁ below the words, are present. Again, in the verse:

In the brìght Mùse, though thòusand chàrms conspìre,

there are five accents, though every accent does not control a foot or unit of two syllables. There are two accents in the consecutive words "bright Muse," and there is none in the two consecutive words preceding,

A   6

though the wave-crest of the metre passes below the second of those two words. Further, in the verse:

And tèn lòw wòrds oft crèep in òne dùll lìne:

there are seven accents; five on the wave-crests of the metre, and two over intermediate wave-troughs, making heavy units like those already discussed at pp. 42 and 49 of the Lyric, so that the last quoted verse contains units similar to those in the line:

The gòod whỳte brède, the gòod rèd wỳne;

and were this line made an Heroic by the addition of a unit:

The gòod whỳte brède and èke the gòod rèd wỳne

it would be a parallel to the one from Pope, and might have been added by him as commentary to the text:

And ten low words oft creep in one dull line,
The good whyte brede and eke the good red wyne.

The fact is, the rules to be observed in the Heroic were too arbitrary, and the units of the end-stopped Heroic vary in much the same way as the units of the Lyric.

Besides the many variations in the individual units of the quotation from Pope, there are two others that concern the full verses. At verse 341, the couplet swells to a triplet. This is a common variation, intended as a relief from the inevitable monotony of the regularly two-syllabled couplet; but so that readers might not be taken unawares, it was found expedient to call attention to the triplet by means of a brace, and a broad-faced brace seemed preferred:

Waller was smooth; but Dryden taught to join⎫
The varying verse, the full resounding line,⎬
The long majestic march, the energy divine.⎭

Upon this Dr Johnson in his *Life of Dryden* observes,
"...the English Alexandrine breaks the lawful bounds,
and surprises the reader with two syllables more than
he expected. The effect of the Triplet is the same;
the ear has been accustomed to expect a new rhyme
at every couplet, but is on a sudden surprised with
three rhymes together, to which the reader could not
accommodate his voice, did he not obtain notice of the
change from the braces of the margins. Surely there
is something unskilful in the necessity of such mechanical direction." Leigh Hunt, on the other hand,
was an admirer of the triplet and the accompanying
brace;—"two lines needlessly extended to three? no;
three lines saying what might have taken four....
I confess I like the very bracket that marks out the
triplet to the reader's eye, and prepares him for the
music of it. It has a look like the bridge of a lute."

The second variation is the one referred to by
Dr Johnson, the swelling of an Heroic verse to an
Alexandrine, as in verses 357 and 373 above; and the
smoothness with which the Lyric combines with the
Heroic shews that they must have some characteristic
in common. The combination is still more musical and
natural when it closes batches of the Heroic broken
into stanza forms with interwoven rimes as in Spenser's
Faerie Queene.

The lyric nature of the Heroic is revealed in other
ways. The Alexandrine inserted may be a full Ballad
verse, and may form one of the verses of a triplet:

> The fanning wind upon her bosom blows,
> To meet the fanning wind the bosom rose,
> The fanning wind, the purling stream, continue her repose.
>
> (Dryden, *Cymon and Iphigenia*, v. 104.)

This verse, says Leigh Hunt, "is peculiar to Dryden, and was taken by him from the lyric poets of his day. So was the Alexandrine itself, and the triplet." Again, the Heroic verse is in structure often near an Alexandrine, as may repeatedly be gathered from Pope:

> List ye sylphs and sylphids, to your chief give ear,
> Fays, fairies, genii, elves and demons, hear!
> Well ye know the spheres, and various tasks assign'd
> By the laws eternal to the aerial kind.
> Some within the fields of purest ether play,
> Rest and bask and whiten in the blaze of day;
> Some guide the course of wandering orbs on high,
> Others roll the planets through the boundless sky;
> Some, less refined, beneath the moon's pale light
> Swift pursue the stars that shoot athwart the night.

Here a few consecutive verses from *The Rape of the Lock* (Canto 2, v. 73 *et seq.*) have been taken, and by the addition of one syllable Heroics have been changed to paused Alexandrines. Such a change is possible in Pope's verses because the caesura often occupies a monotonously regular position, at times following the second unit in many consecutive verses. In the above, three verses out of ten are quite unaltered; and once the new rhythm has been perceived still less need be altered. There are scores upon scores of verses in Pope that need but a pause between the first and second syllables to transform them into paused Alexandrines; there are over two score in the first canto of *The Rape of the Lock*, a canto of less than a hundred and fifty verses.

It may be as well to shew a couple of the above verses marked with the stress-units:

Lìst ye sỳlphs and sỳlphids,   to your chìef give eàr,

Fàys, fàiries, gènii,   èlves and dèmons, hèar!

The Alexandrine lilt of the second verse is particularly clear; in both the mid-pause is unmistakable. It has been thought advisable to shew the units, because to some ears the Alexandrine, when syllabically irregular, has the rhythm of the Heroic metre. For instance, in the second verse above, the hover that lengthens the sound of the word 'Fays' before the first syllable of 'fairies' is uttered, is by some either unheard or disregarded. Instead of

they hear

Fàȳs, fàiries, gĕnii,......

Fȧys, fàiries, gĕnii,......

where the first word, whilst it has an accent, has no metrical stress. The elimination of the hover has the effect of converting two units into one, and consequently, since the mid-pause of the Alexandrine is at the same time shortened to a simple caesura, of converting the Alexandrine into an Heroic verse.

The remarks of Professor Saintsbury in his *Manual* (p. 128) will make this clearer. He says, "Some measures of recent poets have been objected, or at least proposed, as offering difficulties in respect of the system of this book. It has therefore seemed well to scan them here." He quotes from Frederic Myers's *St Paul*:

Yēs, wĭth|out: cheer | of: sis|ter: or | of: daugh|ter—
  Yēs, wĭth|out: stay | of: fa|ther: or | of: son—
Lōne ŏn | the land | and home|less on | the water
  Pāss Ĭ | in pa|tience till | the work | be done.

He then remarks, "There is nothing very peculiar or at all original in all this, though it was probably now first used continuously for a poem of some length. It is only decasyllabic quatrain with uniform redundance in the first and third lines, and a strong inclination to trochaic opening, which in its turn suggests a primary dactyl and trochees to follow, as an alternative (see dotted scansion). Examples of it anterior to Myers may be found—commented on in the larger *History* (vol. III. p. 481)—in *Zophiel*, very likely known to Myers...." On p. 378 of the *History* he quotes a parallel stanza from Emily Brontë's *Remembrance*:

> Cold in the earth, and the deep snow piled above thee,
> Far, far removed, cold in the dreary grave;
> Have I forgot, my only love, to love thee,
> Severed at last by Time's all-severing wave?

"The prosodic scheme," he again says, "is...iambic five foot quatrain with redundance in the odd lines. Miss Brontë, indeed, has perhaps disguised this from very careless folk by admitting a substituted trisyllabic foot in the first line of the first and second stanzas, as well as once or twice elsewhere....Miss Brontë has happened, rather because of her subject than of anything else, to make a strong caesura at the fourth syllable; and she repeats it often, but not invariably or in such a way as to impose it on the ear...." The *Zophiel* stanza by Mrs Brooks has a similar structure:

> So many a soul o'er life's drear desert faring,
>   Love's pure congenial spring unfound—unquaffed,—
> Suffers, recoils, then thirsty and despairing
>   Of what it would, descends and sips the nearest draught.

This Professor Saintsbury calls "a pure prosodic wind-
fall, arising from the adoption of redundant syllables and
double rhymes, which the lady (though a rather bold
experimenter, as her Alexandrine in the text shews,
and as is also shewn by the constant extension of her
quatrain to five, six, or even seven lines) rarely tried
elsewhere, and never successfully." He also quotes a
stanza of *Hark! hark! my soul!* as of parallel structure.

Is it possible that in the reading of these stanzas
no echo sounded in Professor Saintsbury's mind of
Mackay's *Cheer, boys! cheer!*?

> Cheer, boys! cheer! no more of idle sorrow,
>   Courage, true hearts, shall bear us on our way!
> Hope points before, and shows the bright to-morrow,
>   Let us forget the darkness of to-day!

This is no "decasyllabic quatrain" or "five foot quatrain with redundance in the odd lines." To be sure, it
is possible to scan the third and fourth verses so:

> Hòpe pòints befòre, and shòws the brìght to-mòrrow,
>   Lèt ùs forgèt the dàrkness of to-dày!

but the second verse does not fall into this scheme
readily, unless 'courage' is given Chaucer's pronunciation; and the first verse is quite refractory. The cue
is given, indeed, in the hymn quoted by Professor
Saintsbury; each verse is sung as a full lyric verse.
Mackay's stanza, too, is a lyric stanza:

> Chēer, bōys! chēer!   no mòre of ìdle sòrrow,
>   Cŏurăge, trūe hēarts,   shall bèar us òn our wày!
> Hōpe   pòints bĕfòrē,   and shòws the brìght to-mòrrow,
>   Lēt ŭs fŏrgēt   the dàrkness of to-dày!

The spaces shew the hovers, where syllables have been dropped, the wider spaces at the mid-verse shew where a full unit has been dropped—so far as syllables are concerned—as it might be:

Cheer my boys! oh cheer my boys! no more of idle sorrow,

The verses are simply Alexandrines, "equivalenced with monosyllabic feet," to use the terminology of Professor Saintsbury. Miss Brontë's verses are similarly divided:

Cŏld ĭn thĕ earth, and the dèep snòw pĭled abòve thee,
Far, fắr rĕmòved, còld in the drèary gràve;
Have Ĭ fŏrgòt, my ònly lòve, to lòve thee,
Sĕvered ăt làst by Tĭme's àll-sèvering wàve?

The reason is now seen why Miss Brontë "has happened...to make a strong caesura at the fourth syllable"; she felt that the Alexandrine caesura came at that place; and the "substituted trisyllabic foot" has, perhaps, disguised the fact from some very careless folk.... The stanza from *Zophiel* is similar:

Sŏ mắnў ă sòul o'er lĭfe's drèar dèsert fàring,
Lòve's pŭre cŏngènial sprĭng unfòund—unquàffed,—
Sŭffers, rĕcòils, then thĭrsty and despàiring
Ŏf whắt ĭt wŏuld, dĕscènds and sĭps the mèanest dràught.

And here, in the fourth verse, the "bold experimenter" has made the bold experiment of giving the basic verse of her stanza without variation; she has filled the hovers with the dropped syllables.

The strong caesura that Professor Saintsbury finds after the fourth syllable of Miss Brontë's verses is the Alexandrine caesura that divides the verse into two equal halves. The caesura here, as has been shewn, is the equivalent of a dropped unit, and, as is the habit of soundless units that occur between units that are sounded, it suffers compression, so that the mid-pause need not necessarily be of the temporal value of the other units of the verse; it is simply a decided hover, but a hover that may at any time be filled with a unit of one, two, or three syllables.

Particular stress has been given to the scansion of these stanzas because they form the intermediary, the bridge, between the lyric measures and the heroic measures. The fact that Professor Saintsbury scans them as Heroic makes it certain that a great many people will and do regard them as Heroic; but in view of the above scansions is it not clear that they may also be regarded as Lyric? It is all a matter of dropped syllables and hovers; and once the actuality of these is perceived, the actuality of the lyric is also perceived.

One stanza more may be quoted to shew the filling, not only of the hovers where syllables have been dropped, but of the mid-pause where a unit has been dropped. The stanza is the first of C. Kingsley's *The Dead Church*:

Wild wild wind, wilt thou never cease thy sighing?
   Dark dark night, wilt thou never wear away?
Cold cold church, in thy death sleep lying,
   The Lent is past, thy Passion here, but not thine Easter-day.

Here the Alexandrine caesura is clearly shewn by the break at the comma in every verse, the first three words

of the first three lines being equivalents of the single-syllabled units in the lyric line *Love's Young Dream.*
They are also parallels of the opening words of Lord
Bowen's *Shadow Land*:

> Here great souls in a plenitude of vision,
>   Planned high deeds as immortal as the sun;

There is yet another means of transition from the
Heroic to the Lyric, as shewn in Mrs Hemans's *Roman
Girl's Song*:

> Rome, Rome! thou art no more
>   As thou hast been!
> On thy seven hills of yore
>   Thou satt'st a queen.
> Thou hadst thy triumphs then
>   Purpling the street,
> Leaders and sceptred men
>   Bowed at thy feet.

Here the lines are of three and two stresses alternately,
not four and three as in the common Lyric, so that it
would appear that the stanzas are Heroics written in
Lyric form:

> Rome, Rome! thou art no more as thou hast been!
> On thy seven hills of yore thou satt'st a queen.

This is an unexceptionable Heroic couplet, similar in
construction to those quoted from Pope above. As in
Pope's verses, too, the heavy opening unit, "Rome,
Rome!" invites division into two units; and this, with a
pause after 'art,' converts the verse to an Alexandrine:

> Ròme, Ròme! thŏu àrt   no mòre as thòu hast bèen!
> Òn thy sèven hĭlls   of yòre thou sàtt'st a quèen.

This, too, makes a couplet with rhythm as beautiful
as the Heroic couplet. The second stanza, however,

is intractable; it refuses to take on the Alexandrine rhythm whilst it takes on that of the Heroic gracefully enough:

Thòu hadst thy trìumphs thēn   pùrpling the strèet,
Lèaders and scèptred   mēn   bòwed at thy fèet.

Here, however, a curious tendency is seen. The dactylic flow of the syllables 'Thou hadst thy,' and 'purpling the' in the first verse, and 'Leaders and,' and 'bowed at thy' in the second, weakens the accent on 'then' and 'men,' so that there is a tendency to subdue the accent and obliterate the stress at those two words, making 'trìumphs then' and 'scèptred men' dactylic in flow like the words preceding and succeeding:

Thòu hadst thy trìumphs then pùrpling the strèet,
Lèaders and scèptred men bòwed at thy fèet.

Again there has been a metamorphosis; the hovers on 'then' and 'men' have disappeared, verses of five stresses have become lines of four stresses; unusual Heroic has become lilting three-syllabled Lyric; and the metamorphosis, when it is perceived, gives a sensation of delight.

There is a stanza which has long been quoted as an example of alternative rhythm:

I feed a flame within,
    Which so torments me,
That it both pains my heart,
    And yet contents me:
'Tis such a pleasing smart,
    And I so love it,
That I had rather die,
    Than once remove it.

This will read either as Heroic:

> Ì fèed a flàme withìn, which sò tormènts me,
> That ìt bòth pàins my hèart, and yèt contènts me:

or as three-syllabled Lyric:

> Ì feed a flàme within, whìch so tormènts me,
> Thàt it bòth pàins my heart, ànd yet contènts me:

So too, a stanza of Browning's *A Woman's Last Word*
may be read as staccato Heroic:

> Bè a gòd and hòld me
> Wìth a chàrm!
> Bè a màn and fòld me
> Wìth thine àrm!

or as legato and passionate four-syllabled Lyric:

> Bè a gǫd and hòld me wįth a chàrm!
> Bè a mąn and fòld me wįth thine àrm!

There is a passage in Shakespeare that bears on the
question of the blending of the Heroic with the Alexandrine. It occurs in *Love's Labour's Lost.* Jaquenetta
has handed a paper to Sir Nathaniel, desiring him to
read it: Holofernes, the pedantic schoolmaster, catches
a glimpse of the writing, and exclaims, "What, my soul,
verses?" "Ay, sir, and very learned," says Nathaniel.
"Let me hear a staff, a stanza, a verse," exclaims
Holofernes. The stanza is a composition of fourteen
verses, a sonnet, but for the fact that it is written in
paused Alexandrines. It concludes:

> All ignorant that soul, that sees thee without wonder,—
> Which is to me some praise, that I thy parts admire:
> Thy eye Jove's lightning bears, thy voice his dreadful thunder,
> Which, not to anger bent, is music and sweet fire.
> Celestial as thou art, O, pardon love this wrong,
> That sings heaven's praise with such an earthly tongue!

On the verses being read Holofernes immediately remarks, "You find not the apostrophas, and so miss the accent." The verses appear as above, except as regards spelling, in the Folio of 1623; but in some modern editions the last verse is altered, either to "That sings the heaven's praise..." or "That singeth heaven's praise...." This alteration converts an Heroic verse into a paused Alexandrine; and it will be noted that in the Folio it is the only Heroic verse in the quasi-sonnet. It almost seems as if Shakespeare intended the last verse to be different from the rest; intended it as a trap, and Sir Nathaniel was caught, as was at once perceived and remarked by Holofernes. Had that astute schoolmaster been given the reading he would doubtless have avoided the trap by reading 'sings' to its old dissyllabic value ' singes'; he would have perceived that the dropped 'e' lacked its apostrophe. It is more than curious that the presence or absence of a single letter should be able to change the metrical construction of a verse in so remarkable a manner, or perhaps it were better to say, should be able to give the cue to the reader's metrical instinct so unmistakably, for the two constructions lie perdu in the verse itself.

More may be said about three-syllabled units and one-syllabled units occurring in Heroic metre when Blank Verse is being discussed. A few remarks must now be made about the run-on form of the Heroic Couplet. This breaks away more and more from the definiteness of the lyric form, so that the metamorphoses to lyric are not seen in it as definitely as they are in the end-stopped form used by Pope. The running over of the thought from verse to verse, was, as hinted in the triplet above (p. 82), encouraged by Dryden, though he did not originate it, nor is he the only one of the older poets who encouraged it. As is said by Professor Saintsbury, neither form, end-stopped or run-on couplet, is the elder brother; the tendency towards both is already perceived in Chaucer. Waller is reputed to have made the smoothest couplet, that is, his verses tended to be regularly two-syllabled, regularly accented, and regularly end-stopped. The two forms developed side by side, some poets favouring the one, some the other. Of the two, the end-stopped form acquired the more definiteness, and hence was the more favoured for didactic purposes, its definiteness making it very suitable for epigram and antithesis; here, too, rime found its greatest power of emphasis. The reason for the less perfect development of the run-on couplet is partly the loss of the power of the rime through immersion, partly the fact that this is not a final form in itself, it being rather a half-way form in the evolution of Blank Verse.

Rime clinched the couplet, emphasized the verse-ends and the thought-ends. When, then, the thought wished to sweep on unconfined by the limits imposed by the rime, overflowing from verse to verse, shortening but never quite obliterating the verse-end pauses, the first thing that happened was the weakening of the rime. Moreover, in addition to the begetting of its own natural and legitimate sweetness, the rime is apt to beget a wandering voice of thought alien to the nest of song from which it springs. This is referred to by Butler in his couplet (*Hudibras*, Part I, can. I, lines 463–4):

> For rhyme the rudder is of verses,
> With which, like ships, they steer their courses.

The rime has this power in virtue of being at the verse-end, and at a definite break in the thought. If it lose this position, as it does when the verse-end is obscured by the thought running on, making verse-ends at irregular intervals and in indefinite places, it loses much of its power. Indeed, its power becomes an obstruction, imposing limits where none is desired; and it is first immersed, and finally swept away. This immersion and weakening is well shewn in Browning's *Sordello* (Book II, lines 42 etc.):

> In truth
> No prophecy had come to pass: his youth
> In its prime now—and where was homage poured
> Upon Sordello?—born to be adored,
> And suddenly discovered weak, scarce made
> To cope with any, cast into the shade
> By this and this. Yet something seemed to prick
> And tingle in his blood; a sleight—a trick—
> And much would be explained. It went for naught—
> The best of their endowments were ill bought
> With his identity.

Here, when it is noticed at all, the rime seems enervated and impoverished; there is no desire to dwell on it since the thought still calls. It is only when the thought rounds off in the rime that its full richness of detaining sound is appreciated. In *Sordello* the rime seems a superfluity; a wasted ornament; how different from its charm in *The Flight of the Duchess*, or even in *My Last Duchess*, where the running-on, though present, is not so pronounced.

The lyric quality of the Heroic is almost lost in the running-on; how much the Lyric itself suffers if the

lines are allowed to run on is seen in Browning's
Reverie (stanzas 16–19):

> Power is known infinite;
>   Good struggles to be—at best
> Seems—scanned by the human sight,
>   Tried by the senses' test—
> Good palpably: but with right
>
> Therefore to mind's award
>   Of loving, as power claims praise?
> Power, which finds naught too hard,
>   Fulfilling itself all ways
> Unchecked, unchanged: while barred,
>
> Baffled, what good began
>   Ends evil on every side.
> To Power submissive man
>   Breathes "E'en as Thou art, abide!"
> While to good "Late-found, long-sought,
>
> "Would Power to a plenitude
>   But liberate, but enlarge
> Good's strait confine,—renewed
>   Were ever the heart's discharge
> Of loving!" Else doubts intrude.

Where are the beauties of the flowing Lyric? Gone, all
are gone, the old familiar faces. Eventually, rime disappeared, and Blank Verse emerged.

Side by side with the run-on Blank, however, another
form persisted, at any rate for a time, where the pause
was still observed though the rime had been discarded:
an example follows, from Rowe (*The Fair Penitent*,
I. I. 276 *et seq.*):

> Sure 'tis the very error of my eyes!
> Waking I dream, or I behold Lothario;
> He seem'd conferring with Calista's woman:
> At my approach they started and retir'd.

What business could he have here, and with her?
Ha! To Lothario!—'Sdeath! Calista's name!
(Reads the dropped letter.)
The lost indeed! for thou art gone as far
As there can be perdition. Fire and sulphur!
Hell is the sole avenger of such crimes.
Oh, that the ruin were but all thy own!
Thou wilt even make thy father curse his age:
At sight of this black scroll, the gentle Altamont
(For oh! I know his heart is set upon thee)
Shall droop and hang his discontented head,
Like merit scorn'd by insolent authority,
And never grace the public with his virtues.
What if I gave this paper to her father?

These ragged verses are far from the crisp Heroic;
far from the flowing Blank; they are linked to the
former by their end-stopped character, to the latter by
their rimelessness, but they belong to neither. They
attempt to compromise, and fail altogether to please.
The sentences are monotonously and unnaturally regular in length owing to the heroic verse still persisting,
but the verse-ends are tatterdemalion owing to the
check of the rime no longer persisting. They convey
the work of youths and novices, or of older craftsmen
feeble in technique and incapable of the perfect blank.

It has been pointed out by Professor Saintsbury
and others that the earliest Blank Verse in English is
written as prose, in Chaucer's *Tale of Melibeus*; so
that Surrey, the first recognized writer in the metre,
did no more than give its characteristic form to a
metre that already lay incorporated in English litera-
ture. Set out as Blank Verse, the following is the
passage from the Tale:

A   7

> This Melibeus answerede anoon and sayde:
> 'What man' quod he, 'schuld of his wepynge stynte,
> that hath so gret a cause for to wepe?
> Jhesu Crist, oure Lord, him self
> wepte for the deth of Lazarus his frend.'
> Prudens answerede: 'Certes, wel I wot
> attemperel wepyng is no thing defended
> to him that sorwful is, amonges folk in sorwe,
> but it is rather graunted him to wepe.
> The apostel Poule unto the Romayns writeth,
> a man shall rejoyce with hem that maken joye,
> and wepe with such folk as wepen.'

This brings us again to the opening of the first chapter of this book, where it was seen that a passage from Byron, written as prose, is read and perceived as prose; but written as Blank Verse, is as readily perceived and read as Blank Verse.

An examination of a familiar Verse of Blank may shew what it is that so changes the rhythm of the words according as they are regarded as prose or verse.

> Of man's first disobedience, and the fruit

To many, the scansion of this verse as five ordinary two-syllabled units, whilst a little irregular in the placing of the accents, seems regular enough:

> Of màn's fìrst dìsobèdience, ànd the frùit

To others, however, this scansion seems unnatural; too little prominence is given to the important word 'first,' too much to the less important word 'and'; and they would scan it:

> Of màn's‾ fìrst disobèdience, and the frùit

hovering on the liquid of 'man's,' the hover taking the place of the first syllable of the second unit and transferring that syllable to the third, which is in consequence made a unit of three syllables; further, they would obliterate the accent on 'and.'

Here, however, the first storm of opposition arises; two violations of the prosodic law regarding verse-structure have taken place; the second unit has but one syllable, the third has three, and both should have two, no less, no more.

It may be asked, however, who laid down the rule that every unit must have two syllables?—the prosodists? or the poets upon whose works the rules of the prosodists are based?—for as there must be perfected language before there can be any theory of grammar, so there must be perfected poetry before there can be any theory of prosody.

It is doubtful if the poets themselves could explain why they used some units in preference before others. It is certain that they varied the units in an infinite number of ways, and it is this very infinity of variation that causes the dissensions among prosodists, one reading a verse one way, another reading it another way, and neither may be the reading the poet intended. There need not, however, be dissension because of that; all readings may be right, provided only that all conform to one general underlying principle. In short, the *metre* must be the same; the *rhythm* floating on that metre may be as diverse as the natures of the readers.

One may therefore read Milton's verse as regularly two-syllabled units; another may read it with one syllable only in the second unit, and three syllables in the third. Yet another may object that the 'and' still has too much prominence and read the verse:

Of màn's   first disobèdience,   and the frùit

making two units of one syllable each and two of three syllables, the one-syllabled units differing from each other in one having dropped the unaccented syllable, the other the accented syllable.

Here a second and more violent storm of opposition may arise; if it were wrong to drop a syllable from one unit and add it to the next, it were doubly wrong to drop two syllables. Further, two units are now three-syllabled; and of the five units in the verse, four are irregular; only one, the first, conforms to the two syl-labled type-unit of Blank and Heroic verse. The verse, it has been said, is now sheer prose.

It is, however, far from being prose. There is a hover on the liquid consonant of 'man's' that sonantly bridges the gap, really only slight, between 'man's' and 'first'; there is likewise a hover on the liquid (rather than the sibilant, of '-ience' that sonantly bridges the gap be-tween that word-end and 'and.' These hovers preserve the five units of the verse, and preserve their temporal equality. The fact that the accent of the fourth unit has been dropped does not destroy the actuality of that accent as a metrical stress; it is *felt* during the sonant hover in the same way that it is felt in Burns's line already quoted:

> I hànker   and cànker   to sèe their cùrsed prìde.

If the hovers be not observed, the verse takes on the hurry of the Lyric; and the above, read without the hovers, would pair with a lyric line as under:

> For the wày of the wòrld is the ròot
> Of màn's fìrst disobèdience, and the frùit

where the units are the same temporally, though the third unit of the second line has four syllables against the three of the same unit of the first line.

The essential, then, in Blank Verse, is that every verse should have its five temporal units; the distribution of the words—that is, the audible rhythm—may be according to the ear and the feeling of the reader; which means that its variety is infinite and unpredictable.

Milton's verse may therefore read:

> Of màn's first dìsobèdience, ànd the frùit
> *or* Of màn's first dìsobèdience, and the frùit
> *or* Of màn's   first disobèdience, and the frùit
> *or* Of màn's   first disobèdience,   and the frùit

where it will be observed that the temporal units, marked by the ˌ below the words or hover, are five in number always, and temporally are approximately equal; but the words, and the syntactical accents, are very differently distributed. It is this freedom of rhythm, besides the fact that the verse always contains five units, that is the distinguishing characteristic of Blank Verse. It is this that gives scope for the poet's individuality of rhythmic expression. It is also this that constitutes its danger; its liberty is often taken for licence, and the penalty of licence is prose. A poet can suffer no greater.

It has been noted (*see* pp. 49–51) that there are units similar to 'Of màn's first' that have a potentiality to become either Lyric or Blank according as there is not or is a hover between the two accented words. For instance, the verse:

> A mind not to be changed by place or time

is Lyric or Blank according as the verse is read:

> A mìnd nòt to be chànged by plàce or tìme

> *or* A mìnd nòt to be chànged by plàce or tìme

It may of course be read:

> A mìnd not to be chànged by plàce or tìme

and whilst some may read it so, many more will read
it in one of the alternative ways above. There are five
accents in both the alternatives; there are five stresses
only in the second, which is Blank, four in the first, which
is Lyric with a heavy three-syllabled opening unit.

Units with like extra accents often occur in Blank:

> Now I see 'tis true;
> For the blòod-bòlter'd Bànquo smìles upòn me,
> And points at them for his.

> <div align="right">(<i>Macb.</i>, 4, 1, 122-24.)</div>

> so swift with tempest fell
> On the pròud crèst of Sàtan, that nò sìght,
> Nor mòtion of swìft thòught, lèss còuld his shìeld,
> Such ruin intercept.

> <div align="right">(<i>P. L.</i>, 6, 190-93.)</div>

In the units 'For the blòod-bò...,' the first has two
words both unaccented, the second has two words both
accented. Similarly, of Milton's verses, in the units
'On the pròud crèst,'...'tan, that nò sìght,' and ...'tion
of swìft thòught'; the words of the first unit are both
unaccented, the words of the second unit are both
accented. So far from the stresses always coinciding
with the accents, it will be observed that in all of these
units there is an accent that has no stress, and an
unaccented syllable that has a stress. The stresses
accompanying the accents, however, are actual; those

accompanying the unaccented syllables are potential; they are latent only; they are felt, but not heard; that is, the wave-crest of the underflowing metre is felt to pass beneath the unaccented words, whilst the wave-trough is felt to pass beneath the accented words preceding the stress.

Should it be desired, for the sake of emphasis or for any other reason, that all the accents should ride a crest, there is no objection to their doing so:

> For the blòod-   bòlter'd Bànquo smìles upòn me,
> On the pròud   crèst of Sàtan, that nò   sìght,
> Nor mòtion of swìft   thòught ...

Here the words that had accent only have been reinforced with stress, the unaccented words being absorbed in the preceding unit, making it three-syllabled, at the same time losing their position over the potential stress which has now become actual. There has been another element introduced; a sonant hover now comes between the two neighbouring accented words, so that the two units, instead of consisting, as they did, of a unit with two unaccented syllables, followed by one with two accented syllables, consist of a unit of three syllables, the third stressed, followed by one composed of a hover and a stressed syllable. Whilst, therefore, the two words which were accented and adjacent are now both stressed, whereas previously only the second was stressed, they are no longer actually adjacent; there is a time-space between them, that space being bridged by the hover. This fact emerges; the wave-crests, which coincide with the stresses, do not change their relative positions; it is the position of the syllables floating upon them that is changed. From this it is evident that whilst accented syllables may come together with no hover between them, stressed syllables may not. The juxtaposition of accented syllables has caused endless disputation among prosodists, ancient and modern; Dr Guest would disallow it if he could; Dr Johnson admits its possibility with apparent grudging; Professor Saintsbury admits it as a spondee.

Whilst the contiguity of the syllables may be avoided as above, if desired, units occur where it cannot be avoided:

> Thus at their shady lodge arriv'd, bòth stòod,
> Bòth tùrn'd, and under open sky ador'd
>
> (*P. L.*, 4, 720-21.)

Nor is there any necessity for avoiding it: though the construction does not often run to the length of:

> Hò! hèarts, tòngues, fìgures, scrìbes, bàrds, pòets, cànnot
> Thìnk, spèak, càst, wrìte, sìng, nùmber—hò!
> His love to Antony.
>
> (*Ant. and Cleo.*, 3, 2, 16-18.)

Such units as these, besides the more familiar one of the progress of Satan in Milton, cannot be ignored. Speaking of the two units in the quotation from *Paradise Lost* above, Dr Johnson suggested that the accent is equally strong on the two adjoining syllables; but Dr Guest objects, "every reader of taste would pronounce the words *stood, turn'd,* with a greater stress, than that which falls upon the words preceding them. But these words are at least equal to them in *quantity*; and Johnson fell into the mistake, at that time so prevalent, of considering quantity as identical with accent....Surely every one would throw a stronger

accent on the first syllable than on the second." In the
last sentence Dr Guest seems to contradict himself;
but in his first remark, that the words 'stood' and
'turn'd' have a greater stress than the words preceding
them, that is than the word 'both,' he is correct. Nor is
Dr Johnson incorrect; the *accent* is equally strong on
the adjacent words, but the second word in both cases
rides in addition on the wave-crest, which reinforces the
accent, making it a stress; so that the sole difference
between Dr Johnson and Dr Guest is, that Dr Guest
felt that the second word of each pair carries more
weight, though he might not *hear* it; Dr Johnson neither
felt it nor heard it.

The two accented words may precede the two unaccented words instead of following them:

For òne restràint, lòrds òf the wòrld besìdes?

(*P. L.*, 1, 32.)

It will be observed that there is here a strong tendency
to do one of two things; either to shift the stress from
the fourth syllable, which bears an accent, to the fifth,
which also bears an accent, or else to cause the word
'lords' to usurp the accent and stress of the word 'of,'
inducing a hover between 'restraint' and 'lord':

For òne restràint, lòrds of the wòrld besìdes?

For òne restràint, lòrds of the wòrld besìdes?

In the former reading the Blank has lost a stress and
become Lyric, a parallel to Shelley's line:

To ròof the glòw-wòrms from the èvening dèw

(*Sens. Plant*, pt. 1, 1, 57.)

while in the second the result is as in the units of
'On the pròud crèst of Sàtan...,' except that now the

unit of three syllables follows the unit of hover and syllable instead of preceding it:

> For òne restràint, lòrds of the wòrld besìdes?
> On the pròud crèst of Sàtan, that nò sìght
> *or* On the pròud crèst of Sàtan, that nò sìght

In the present instance, too, there is a much greater tendency towards making the hover, as if the stress will tolerate an accented syllable immediately before it, but is less tolerant of one immediately following.

Units identical with 'lords of the world' occur very frequently at the opening of the verse:

> Hòvering on wìng ùnder the còpe of hèll
> (*P. L.*, 1, 35.)
> Squàt like a tòad, clòse at the èar of Ève,
> (*P. L.*, 4, 800.)
> Mòors by his sìde ùnder the lèe, while nìght
> Invests the sea,
> (*P. L.*, 1, 207-8.)

In these quotations there are two of these pairs of units in the three verses. It has been said by prosodists that in units like the opening units of the three verses above, an inversion of rhythm has taken place; trochee precedes iamb, instead of iamb preceding iamb as is usual in the Heroic or Blank rhythm. Calling the opening "trochaic-iambic" preserves the two syllables in each unit:

Squat like/ a toad

Professor Saintsbury divides the units in this way; but how is it to be known that the above is not intended to be read:

Squat lìke/ a tòad

the accents falling regularly on the second syllables of the units?

Moreover, no note has been taken of the decided pause preceding opening units such as the above:

> He ended frowning, and his look denounc'd
> Desp'rate revenge, and battle dangerous
> To less than gods.
>
> *(P. L.,* 2, 106-8.)

There is no denying that the hover between 'denounc'd' and 'desp'rate' is of a different kind from the one between 'dangerous' and 'to'; it is much more sustained; it includes, in fact, not only the usual verse-end hover, but also a hover equal to the time-value of a dropped syllable; and such syllable may at any time be restored without any hurrying of the rhythm resulting:

> He ended frowning, and his look denounc'd
> A desp'rate revenge,

when the verse-end hover has become normal, the first unit of the second verse also being normal, with a three-syllabled unit following. The effect is the same as the third unit in:

> Your strìnges trùsty and trùe.

> *(A Lytell Geste of Robyn Hode,* fytte 4, st. 11.)

which becomes, in modern verse:

> Your strìngs ‾‾‾ trùsty and trùe.

It is the same construction as in Browning's cavalier song *Marching along*:

> Kentish Sir Byng   stood for his king

Objection is then made that these are in Lyric rhythm, and that many rhythms allowed in Lyric are not allowed in Blank. When, however, Milton's verse is read:

Hòvering on wȉng undèr the còpe of hèll

the pronunciation of 'undèr,' accented on the second syllable, is a Lyric pronunciation. Again, it is said that

Hòvering on wȉng ‾‾ ȕnder the còpe of hèll

is too much like prose rhythm; but again it is far from prose rhythm, for the hover on 'wing' makes the one-syllabled third unit temporally equal to the three-syllabled second and fourth; in fact, makes all five units temporally equal, and this temporal equality is alien to prose.

The "trochaic-iambic" scansion was perhaps adopted to stem the three-syllabled irruption that is otherwise threatened. Three-syllabled units have not now, however, the forbidding aspect they once had. The cult of apostrophation has probably had its day, and Milton for instance will not again be edited as he was edited by Newton. Such verses as:

Retire, or taste thy folly, and learn by proof,

(*P. L.*, 2, 686.)

to many ears have a syllable too many, and the verse was printed:

Retire, or taste thy folly', and learn by proof,

where the apostrophe meant that a vowel was to be elided—the 'y' of 'folly' and the 'a' of 'and' being coalesced—'follyand,' in spite of the syntactical pause indicated by the comma. Newton makes it clear that this was intended, explaining his use of the apostrophe in a note to line 39 of Book I. He says that Milton, to improve and vary his versification, pronounces the same word "sometimes as two syllables, and sometimes as only one syllable or two short ones. We have frequent instances," says he, "in *spirit, ruin, riot, reason, highest*, and several other words. But then these excellencies in Milton's verse are attended with this inconvenience, that his numbers seem embarrassed to such readers as know not, or know not readily, where such elision or abbreviation of vowels is to take place; and therefore for their sake we shall take care throughout this edition to mark such vowels as are to be contracted and abbreviated thus'." A few lines above he has said that Milton "often cuts off the vowel at the end of a word, when the next word begins with a vowel; though he does not like the Greeks wholly drop the vowel, but still retains it in writing like the Latins.' From this it is evident that to him there was nothing objectionable in the sound 'spirt' or 'sprit' for 'spirit,' 'rune' for 'ruin,' 'rite' for 'riot,' 'hist' for 'highest,' though how he could by any means say 'reason' as one syllable is incomprehensible. It is true he has authority for the common elision of the 'e' in 'the'; for in the E.E. Text Society's *O.S.* No. 149, p. 237, appears the following: "To have and to hold...with thappurtenaunces...from the feaste of seincte mighell tharchaungell next cominge...," and 'thinhabitants' has been noted in another document, so that it is evident that the crushing of the words was at one time considered unobjectionable, and it is possible that the elisions actually took place in Milton; that the apostrophated syllables were, as he himself expresses it in another matter,

> thrown out, as supernumerary
> To my just numbers found.

In some instances, however, the apostrophation failed of its purpose, if its purpose were indeed the reduction of redundant syllables:

> bears, tigers, ounces, pards,
> Gàmbol'd befòre them; th' unwȷeldy èlephant,
> To make them mirth, us'd all his might,
>
> (*P. L.*, 4, 344-46.)

Here the device certainly reduces a unit of four syllables to one of three, but it does not make the unit two-syllabled:

> them, th' unwȷel

which seems a dreadful unit to the eye, though the ear accepts it readily enough, even without evisceration of the 'e':

> them, the unwȷel

This, however, is neither Newton's scansion nor Bentley's; for the latter gives the warning, "Mind the accent of *unwieldly* in the first syllable. The author knew the common pronunciation to be in the second, as 7, 411, *Wallowing unwieldy*. But with great art and judgment following his principals Homer and Virgil, he made the verse itself *unwieldy*, that the reader might feel it as well as understand it." A curious rhythm results:

> Gàmbol'd befòre them; th' ùnwieldy èlephant,

which to the writer conveys no impression of unwieldiness, but rather of lyric lightness, and the hurried lightness of the four-syllabled lyric. In spite of the unusual accentuation, too, the second and fourth units are still three-syllabled. The very fact, however, that the reading of Newton and Bentley was found possible to them and no doubt to others, whilst yet others

would propose other and very different readings, shews
how varied is the rhythm that may float on the same
five-unit metre, and how useless it is for any one to
say definitely that the verse should be read in such
and such a way. So long as he observes the five temporal units, the reader may read as it pleases him.
To some, in whom perhaps the underflowing metre
beats faintly, the regular recurrence of accents and the
regular distribution of syllables may be necessary, or
they may prefer the very regularity for its own sake,
even though it be attained by means of apostrophation
or coalescence; to others, keenly alive to the underflowing metre, stresses may be suppressed, syllables
dropped or added, without loss of enjoyment, without
loss of metre, and with gain of extraordinary diversity of rhythm. Of the latter class is a recent writer,
Mr M. A. Bayfield, who in his *Study of Shakespeare's
Versification* would resolve all the apostrophations
with which the pages of Shakespeare are disfigured,
scattering three, four, and even five-syllabled units
through the plays, and the present writer read much
of his book with high approval. Mr Bayfield finds no
less than "844 quadrisyllabics and 18 quinquesyllabics"
in the plays, and there is little doubt that Shakespeare
was aware of them.

There are very many units in Blank Verse that are
divided like the verse of Milton above quoted, the first
syllable of the unit being disconnected syntactically
from the syllable following; and the disconnection may
take place in a unit of two, three, or four syllables:

Strànge hòrror sèize thee, and pàngs unfèlt befòre.

(*P. L.*, 2, 703.)

Syllables such as 'them' in 'Gambol'd before them,' and 'thee' in 'Strange horror seize thee,' have been called supernumerary, or extrametrical, or redundant; they are all these to those who count the syllables; they are none of them to those who count the temporal units; and the poets themselves seem to be in the latter class. Were there no syntactical pause after the words 'them' and 'thee,' the units in which they occur would be ordinary three-syllabled units; and much as these have been condemned by some in the past, it is now generally admitted that their occurrence in the best poetry is not accidental or unavoidable merely, but was actually intentional on the part of the poet, and must therefore be admitted, if not accepted, by the prosodist.

Examples have already been given in the chapter on the stress-unit, shewing how the unit may be broken in any part, be it composed of two, three, or four syllables.

The admission that the verse may contain three-syllabled units carries with it, of course, the admission that it may contain more than ten syllables; how many more depends—simply upon the taste of the poet or the reader. Swinburne, whose ear was musical enough, has a verse with fourteen:

Thou art older and colder of spirit and blood than I.

The last unit may as well have been 'than am I,' when the verse would have contained fifteen syllables, every unit being three-syllabled. Such a verse actually occurs in Calverley, and whilst it is a parody, that does not alter its constitution as a verse:

Of a bit of a chit of a boy i' the mid o' the day.

Eleven or twelve syllables may be conceded without scruple; more are no doubt admissible, but the deliberate Blank is then apt to take on the livelier character of the Lyric; and this, rather than the number of syllables, is the objection to a greater number than an occasional eleven or twelve, or whatever number gives a more suitable rhythm at the moment.

As strong objection is still taken to a verse of less than ten syllables as was once taken to a verse of more than ten. Whilst Milton in *Paradise Lost* has used no verse of less than ten syllables, the writer has, in five different editions of that poem, found nine-syllabled verses, but in every instance the verse has been found to contain a misprint. The following occurs in Newton's 1773 edition—it is altered in the edition of 1790:

> Thither let us bend our thoughts, to learn
> What creatures there inhabit,

(P. L., 2, 354.)

The first verse above contains only nine syllables, and was apparently intended to be:

> Thìther let ùs bend àll our thòughts, to lèarn

altering the rhythm from:

> Thìther lèt us bènd our thòughts, to lèarn.

Some will prefer one rhythm, some the other; both seem unobjectionable. One fact is fairly clear through this correction; even those who prefer extreme regularity would rather admit a three-syllabled unit than a nine-syllabled verse.

Nine-syllabled verses are, however, found from Chaucer onwards. They were also found earlier than

A   8

Chaucer. Guest says of them that they "abound in
Anglo-Saxon; they are also met with in Chaucer and
the writers of the fifteenth century, but were rarely used
after that period, except by our dramatists." A notable
exception. He gives many examples (*A History of
English Rhythms*, 1882, pp. 209 *et seq.*). Bayfield has
collected examples from Shakespeare, and included
them in his list of "pure trochaic pentapodies" (*Shakespeare's Versification*, pp. 315 *et seq.*).

Two good examples may be quoted:

> good uncle, hide such malice;
> Wìth such hòliness can yòu do ìt?

(Part 2 *King Henry VI*, 2, 1, 26.)

> thrice from the banks of Wye
> And sandy-bottom'd Severn have I sent him
> Bòotless hòme and wèather-bèaten bàck.

(Part 1 *King Henry IV*, 3, 1, 66.)

In the Irving Shakespeare the former is amended:

> With so much holiness can you not do it?

and Warburton goes half way, retaining the rhythm
with:

> With such holiness can you not do it?

In the Irving, again, the latter example is amended by
the obvious:

> have I sent
> Him bootless home and weather-beaten back.

This, however, introduces a pause between the words
'sent' and 'him,' where no pause should be. Taken
together, the two verses are perfectly rhythmical, and
they contain twenty syllables between them; is the
ear conscious of any inharmony in the sound of them?

We no longer follow Fadladeen of *Lalla Rookh* who, commenting on the verse:

> Like the faint, exquisite music of a dream,

said, "What critic that can count, and has his full complement of fingers to count withal, would tolerate for an instant such syllabic superfluities?" The syllabic superfluities are now not only tolerated but admired, so long as they are used to vary, not to violate, the rhythm of the Heroic and Blank; may not the syllabic deficiencies be admitted for a like reason?

It is only occasionally that the nine-syllabled verse follows one whose feminine ending makes the tale of twenty syllables to the two verses, as it does in the two above quoted. In the following, the two verses contain only nineteen syllables:

> And strew him with sweet-smelling violets,
> Blushing roses, purple hyacinths:
> > (*The Tragedy of Queen Dido*, 2, 21-2 from end.)

"which should be read," says J. M. in *Gentleman's Magazine* for January 1841,

> "With blushing roses, purple hyacinths:"

but apparently Marlowe did not think so; for in *Tamburlaine* he has:

> Barbarous and bloody Tamburlaine,
> Thus to deprive me of my crown and life!—
> Treacherous and false Theridamas,
> Even at the morning of my happy state,
> . . . .
> Who entering at the breach thy sword hath made,
> Sacks every vein and artier of my heart.—
> Bloody and insatiate Tamburlaine!
> > (First Part of *Tamburlaine the Great*, 2, 7, opening.)

8-2

Here the first and third verses are nine-syllabled, and
the last of the speech was no doubt also considered so;
for a note (Dyce's *Marlowe*) says: "Qy. 'O barbarous'?
in the next line but one, 'O treacherous'? in the last
line of the speech, 'O bloody'? But we occasionally
find in our early dramatists lines which are defective
in the first syllable; and in some of these instances at
least it would almost seem that nothing had been
omitted by the transcriber or printer."

In many instances verses are nine-syllabled or ten-
syllabled according as certain words are used as words
of one or of two syllables:

> My *oars* broken, and my tackling lost
> > (*The Tragedy of Queen Dido*, 3, 106.)
> *Oars* of massy ivory, full of holes
> > (*Ib.* 3, 117.)

In the former the word 'oars' must be given a two-
syllabled value if the verse is to have ten syllables;
in the latter it need not. There are innumerable instances of the kind.

Whilst the nine-syllabled verses of which examples
have so far been quoted seem harmonious enough, and
therefore unexceptionable, there are others that are
more open to question:

> By full consent of all the synod
> Of priests and prelates, it is thus decreed,—
> (*The Tragical History of Doctor Faustus*; p. 120 of Dyce's *Marlowe*.)

In the first verse not only has the last syllable been
dropped, but with it the last stress; and the reading is
inclined to be made:

> By fùll consènt of àll the sỳnod of prìests and prèlates,

instead of:

> By full consent of all the synod of priests,

making the first verse a lyric line parallel to:

> When lovely woman stoops to folly,

Not that the rhythm seems objectionable in itself, but with many such interspersed lines the lyric rhythm would take the place of the more deliberate Blank.

Sometimes a syllable is dropped within the verse:

> wicked dreams abuse
> The curtain'd sleep; witchcraft celebrates
> Pale Hecate's offerings;
>
> (*Macbeth*, 2, 1, 51.)

To avoid the nine syllables, Steevens conjectured that 'sleep' should be 'sleeper'; Sir William Davenant inserted 'now' between 'sleep' and 'witchcraft', and this is adopted in Reed's Shakespeare; but, as Gollancz remarks in the Temple Shakespeare, "no emendation is necessary; the pause after 'sleep' is evidently equivalent to a syllable." Again:

> I learn'd of thee.   How! not dead? not dead?
>
> (*Ant. and Cleo.* 4, 14, 102.)
> And he hath sent for thee: for the queen,
> I'll take her to my guard.
>
> (*Ib.* 5, 2, 65.)

In these examples, no doubt the pause takes the place of a syllable dropped. In the first the pause between the words 'thee' and 'How' would become the syntactical pause merely were the word 'now' inserted after 'How':

> I learn'd of thee, How now! not dead? not dead?

The second line would become one of an accepted
type by insertion of the word 'as' before 'for':

And hè hath sènt for thèe: às for the quèen,

where the verse is given its ten syllables, whilst the
pause after the word 'thee' remains, and 'for' is removed from its position riding the stress where it
received unnatural prominence. These verses, whilst at
first a little baffling, are not altogether inharmonious,
though approaching too near inharmony to be comfortable; but when no pause is indicated as by a
syntactical break, inharmony enters:

Her palfrey swift running as the wind,

which defeats its own end, for it stumbles at the 'swift';
it would not have done so had the word been 'swiftly'.
This is so palpable that Lydgate, the author of the
verse, either heard no inharmony in it, or he himself,
intending 'swift' as an adjective, not as an adverb,
paused naturally between the two words:

Her pàlfrey swìft   rùnning as the wind.

Here, however, he fails in the poet's duty towards his
neighbour, which is to leave no doubt at all of the
rhythm intended. If the structure of a verse ruin the
rhythm or confound the reader, the structure is wrong.
Lydgate has so many of these verses that he impeaches
his own sense of harmony, and Professor Saintsbury
is justified in his truculent denouncing of what he calls
"the detestable Lydgatian breakback, which ruins any
symphony."

Many verses may of course be found whose rhythm
cannot be reconciled to that of Blank, varied as that
may be. In the older drama such rugged verses may

be due to changes in spelling or pronunciation, or
to faulty transmission, that is, they may have been
rhythmical enough when written. A verse like

> Whò can be pàtient ın sùch extrèmes?
> <div align="right">(Part 3 <i>King Henry VI</i>, 1, 1, 216.)</div>

would now, apart from its context, be read as lyric·
It is similar to Gower's line:

> Out of the temple he goth his way,

but in Blank is regular enough when the three-syllabled value of 'patient' is observed:

> Whò can be pàtiènt in sùch extrèmes?

So too, the verse:

> Ì am the sòn of Hènry the Fìfth,

is lyric out of its context, and until it is known that the
name was pronounced both 'Henry' as at present, and
'Henery':

> Ì am the sòn of Hènerỳ the Fìfth.

Again, a sentence like

> Women are soft, mild, pitiful and flexible

though in rhythm prosaic enough, may yet adapt itself
to the five temporal periods, and may adapt itself in
several ways according to the rhythmical sense of the
reader:

> Wòmen are sòft, mìld, pìtiful and flèxible;
> *or* Wòmen are sòft, mìld, pìtifùl and flèxible;
> *or* Wòmen are sòft,   mìld,   pìtiful and flèxible;

the hovers indicated in the last being only slightly
more than those observed in the first two readings.

It is sufficient to indicate that such verses occur; they are neither defended nor condemned, though many would defend them, many would condemn them.

When defining the difference between Lyric and Blank at the opening of the chapter, it was said that the sentences in Lyric break up regularly; that in Blank they break up irregularly; that in Lyric they are confined within the verses; that in Blank they overflow the confine of the verses, running on and ending at any part within a verse.

One result of this running-on is shewn in the fractional verses so common in Shakespeare's dramatic Blank. The sentence continued from one verse may be complete before the end of that verse is reached, and rather than eke out the verse unnecessarily, the verse-norm has been left incomplete. Often, though by no means always, whilst the verse is incomplete the fractional part, taken with part of the verse preceding, makes a complete verse. This is shewn in the following, where the verse-making fractional parts are enclosed in double bars:

> This sword, but shown to Caesar, || with this tidings,
> Shall enter me with him. ||
>
> > > (*Ant. and Cleo.* 4, 14, 112.)
> > > a Roman by a Roman
> Valiantly vanquish'd. || Now my spirit is going;
> I can no more. ||
>
> > > (*Ib.* 4, 15, 58.)
> > > ||Alack, our terrene moon
> Is now eclipsed, || and it portends alone
> The fall of Antony. ||
>
> > > (*Ib.* 3, 13, 153.)

One speech may end in a fractional verse, and the following speech complete it:

    Ant.   Tend me two hours to-night, | I ask no more,
        || And the gods yield you for it! |
    Eno. | What mean you, sir, ||
        To give them this for comfort? |
                            (*Ant. and Cleo.* 4, 2, 32.)

It will be observed that there is here as it were a double completion of the fractional verses; the close of one speech is completed by the short phrase in the verse before, the opening of the other by the longer phrase in the verse following, as shewn by the single bars. More than two speeches may be required to complete the verse.

    Mar. | She render'd life,
        || Thy name so buried in her. |
    Ant.   Dead, then?
    Mar.   Dead. ||
                            (*Ib.* 4, 14, 33.)

    Iras. || She's dead too, our sovereign.
    Char.   Lady!
    Iras.   Madam! ||
                          (*Ib.* 4, 15, 69.)

Whilst Milton allows no fractional verses of this kind in *Paradise Lost,* he allows them by enclosing verses within verses. That is, besides the normal division into verses, the sentences often break so that other verses are formed whose beginnings and ends do not coincide with the verses into which the poem is divided. The result is that two metres arise and blend in a kind of exalted canon, or prosodic counterpoint; and one familiar with the ordinary rhythm of the verses is conscious of a second rhythm emerging and mingling with the ordinary rhythm:

> || Wherefore do I assume
> These royalties, || and not refuse to reign,
> Refusing to accept as great a share
> Of hazard as of honour, due alike
> To him who reigns, || and so much to him due
> Of hazard more, || as he above the rest
> High honour'd sits? || Go therefore mighty Powers,
> Terror of Heav'n, || though fall'n ; || intend at home,
> While here shall be our home, || what best may ease
> The present misery, || and render Hell
> More tolerable ;

>   (*P. L.* 2, 450 *et seq.*)

The latter part of this quotation might be re-arranged:

> And so much to him due of hazard more,
> As he above the rest high honour'd sits?
> Go therefore mighty Powers, terror of Heav'n,
> Though fall'n ;
> Intend at home, while here shall be our home,
> What best may ease the present misery,
> And render Hell more tolerable ;

which shews a dim emergence of verses more akin to those of the Heroic couplet.

A restriction must now be noted. In Blank the thought runs on from verse to verse, but runs on in such a way that the verse-end pause may still be observed; as though the tendency, or rather the necessity, were the preservation of the metrical norm, the verse-unit. The subject-matter, the poetry, dilates or contracts with the glow and gush of emotion, embracing more norms than one, or less than one, proving their plasticity to the utmost, but never confusing them. The slight verse-end hovers or pauses are for the ensuring and securing of the verse-norm; but so far from the thought-sentences being thereby restricted to their average length, they may expand or contract as emotion urges, pausing at any part of the verse, and as often within a verse as they please, provided they allow one of the pauses to coincide with the verse-end. In prose there is no norm, and the incidence of the pause is haphazard, with no restriction whatever. It is the disregard shewn for the end-pause that has caused objection to be taken to the two following verses:

> Ophion, with Eurynome, the wide.
> Encroaching Eve, perhaps,
>
> *(P. L.* 10, 581.)
>
> When, to inshrine his reliques in the sun's
> Bright temple,
>
> *(Ib.* 5, 273.)

The writers of what Professor Saintsbury has called the decadent Blank were either unconscious of the reason for the verse-end pause, or disregarded it; with what results the following quotation shews:

> Rhodolinda doth become her title
> And her birth. Since deprived of popular
> Homage, she hath been queen over her great self,
> In this captivity ne'er passionate
> But when she hears me name the king, and then
> Her passions not of anger taste, but love;
> Love of her conqueror; he that in fierce
> Battle (when the cannon's sulphurous breath
> Clouded the day) her noble father slew.
>
> (Davenant, *Albovine.*)

As Professor Saintsbury says, this is "immedicable"; it is neither Blank nor Prose, but inharmoniously jolts from one to the other. In the quotation from Rowe the verse-end pauses were too much regarded; here they are too little regarded.

Free as Blank is, then, there are subtle restrictions that must be observed if the Blank is not to become Prose, and bad Prose. So long as the words are able to adjust themselves smoothly to the five time-periods, Blank Verse results; if the accents are so irregular in their occurrence as to prohibit adjustment, the words are Prose, so far as the metre is concerned, however exalted they may be in thought and expression. Nor need the adjustment always take place in the same way; the words may be arranged in a different manner by different readers, or in different manner at different times by the same reader. So long as the regularly-recurring time-periods are observed, and the words arranged so that these periods are made evident, the result is Blank Verse.

CHAPTER V

THE STANZA-UNIT

As the stress-unit and the verse-unit appear to be controlled as regards their length and duration by natural functions, the heart-beat and breath respectively, so the length of the stanza appears to be controlled by a third natural function, the thought. The first and simplest stanza appears as the form into which a single thought was cast; and it follows that, as regards length, the first verse and the first stanza, each a single thought, were one and the same thing. Again, as the complete thought is usually composed of two complementary or antithetical clauses, so the primal verse and stanza falls into two equal halves, the whole beating and hovering about the evolving norm the verse of eight units.

This beating and hovering is plainly seen in the old unsmoothed ballads: *Agnes and the Merman*, in Grundtvig's collection of Danish ballads, shews the settling towards the octosyllabic couplet, the Romance metre; the *Ballad of Chevy Chase*, as preserved by Percy, shews the settling towards the ballad metre. In these ballads the thoughts are plain and direct; but as the minds of the singers and listeners became more cultivated, the thoughts became more elaborated; and whilst the verse-unit remained the same in length, the stanza expanded to accommodate the growing thought. The culmination of this expansion is in the sonnet, and sestina, and chant royal, in each of which is expressed a single elaborated thought. This culmination,

however, is not universally appreciated: to a great many
minds these long elaborated stanzas make little appeal,
this remark applying more especially to the artificial
forms of the sestina and chant royal. Even the sonnet
appeals chiefly to readers whose intellect has been
cultivated above the average, and it is curious that the
sonnet has parallels in structure with the ballad verse
itself. The simple ballad verse usually has fourteen
syllables; the sonnet has fourteen verses. The ballad
verse is divided into two unequal parts of eight and
six syllables respectively; the sonnet is divided into
two unequal parts of eight and six verses respectively,
the octave and the sestet. The full thought included
in the ballad verse is usually in two parts, one complementary or antithetical to the other; the thought
in the sonnet is likewise divided, the octave usually
containing the statement of the thought, the sestet its
application. The clause of the first half of the ballad
verse often falls naturally into two sub-clauses; in the
octave of the sonnet the thought is often similarly
twinned. The quick return of rime when the sub-
clauses of the ballad line rime together is paralleled
in the enclosed riming of the octave of the sonnet. All
this may be no more than coincidence, but it would
be strange if there were no parallel between the ballad
verse that has almost universal appeal to all emotional
people, and the sonnet, which has such wide appeal to
the smaller class of people whose emotions may be
a little more controlled by their intellect, but whose
intellect is nevertheless so suffused by their emotions
under the influence of poetry, that they react to the
same metre in another guise.

The appeal of the short lyric stanza is almost universal. Each verse is a thought, each thought is a picture; and as a picture gains definiteness by being framed off from its surroundings, so the thought gains definiteness by being detached in a measure from the surrounding thoughts. In the first verse-pictures, the means of detachment was rime.

The first stanzas, then, are simply riming couplets. In the breaking up, or re-forming, or evolution, of the alliterative stave, there was a trend in two or more directions; one in the direction of the Romance couplet composed of two lines each containing four stress-units, and one in the direction of a couplet composed of longer lines, the Ballad verse, containing seven stress-units that were audible, the eighth, preserving the parallel with the Romance couplet, being dropped, but not lost. These couplets formed the first stanzas, both kinds riming in pairs. The stanza composed of a Romance couplet occurs in such ballads as *Agnes and the Merman*:

> Agnete she stands on the Highland bridge,
> And up came the merman from billows' blue ridge.
>
> As purest gold-glimmer, so was his hair,
> The joy of his heart in his eyes lay bare.

The stanza composed of a pair of Ballad verses occurs very commonly in the old ballads:

> Thes worthè freckys for to fyght
>   therto the wear full fayne,
> Tyll the blood owte off thear basnetes sprente,
>   as ever dyd heal or rayne.

In the old written copy from which the ballad of the *Battle of Chevy Chase* was taken by Hearne (see Percy's

Reliques, vol. I), it was written without any division into stanzas, in long lines. It would be heard so; the rimes marked off certain thoughts, mental pictures, the stanza above quoted being one such picture.

The primary cause of the extension of any stanza was extension of the thought, or addition to the thought; and the simplest extension was by agglutination, two couplets being gathered together, making a stanza of four lines:

> As I was walking all alane,
> I heard twa corbies making a mean;
> The tane unto the t'other gan say,
> "Whaur sall we gang and dine to-day?"

In this stanza, the first couplet presents a complete thought of two clauses, and makes a complete picture. A certain amount of detail is added to the picture by the addition of the second couplet, and whereas the first couplet is independent of the second, the second is not independent of the first. This is a condition of the true stanza; the latter parts should not be independent of the earlier, or the picture itself breaks into parts. When a ballad is recited, the hearers frame their own pictures, make their own stanzas. The transcribers do likewise; and the ballad *Glenlogie* is by Roberts printed in two-lined stanzas, instead of in four-lined stanzas as by other transcribers.

The extreme of the couplet-agglutination appears when the whole ballad or story is printed without any division into stanzas, as in the Metrical Romances; Gower's *Confessio Amantis* and the like. Indeed, it would be difficult to say with certainty that stanzas ever had definite existence in the couplet form of the ballad, though there is no doubt that a series of pictures, definite and varied, was created in the mind as the couplets were recited or sung, and the individualization of the stanza is more or less indicated by the presence of the refrains where such occur.

The couplet-agglutination does not build up true stanzas; the picture is not sufficiently detached from its surroundings. As the verse acquired definiteness, however, the stanza too acquired definiteness, but probably not through the Romance couplet.

Parallel with the trend towards the Ballad verse, where the last unit was dropped, was a trend towards a full Romance verse retaining the last unit, this verse falling into riming couplets similar to the Ballad couplet.

Webbe in his *Discourse* notes that the longest verse he has seen used consists of sixteen syllables, two verses riming together; and he quotes:

> When virtue wants and vice abounds, then wealth is but a
> bayted hooke,
> To make men swallow down their bane, before on danger deep
> they looke.

"This kynde is not very much used at length thus," says he, "but is commonly devided, eche verse, into two, whereof eche shal containe eight syllables, and ryme cross wise, the first to the thyrd, and the second to the fourth, in this manner:

> Great wealth is but a bayted hooke,
> When virtue wants, and vice abounds;
> Which men devoure before they looke,
> So them in danger deepe it drownes."

Ballad metre, he says, "next in length to thys," is also in one line, but "may lykewise and so is often devyded."

A   9

It is this dividing and cross-riming that gives rise to the first true stanza-forms; the rimes knit the whole together, the four lines forming, as Ten Brink observes, the four sides to the frame of the picture contained in the stanza.

As rime clinches two lines into a couplet-stanza, so it may clinch three into a triplet-stanza:

> And here the precious dust is laid,
> Whose purely-tempered clay was made
> So fine, that it its guest betrayed.
>
> (Carew, *An Epitaph.*)

The stanza of four lines so rimed is less common, though not uncommon:

> And would you see my mistris' face?
> It is a flowrie garden place,
> Where knots of beauties have such grace,
> That all is worke, and no where space.
>
> (*The Idea of her Sex*, st. 1.)

This riming may, however, be carried to almost any length, and the result is similar to that in the couplet, the stanza is not coherent, and may be split at almost any part into two or more smaller stanzas; so that the mono-rimed stanza of more than three lines can hardly be considered to be a true unit.

The three-lined stanza is, however, a unit, as it cannot be split into smaller couplet-units; and the four-lined may be made a unit by means of an apparently isolated line:

> How faintly-flushed, how phantom fair,
> Was Monte Rosa, hanging there
> A thousand shadowy pencill'd valleys
> And snowy dells in a golden air.
>
> (Tennyson, *The Daisy*, st. 17.)

The third line may sound a music of its own:

> And this the burden that it bore:
> "No meeting now for evermore;
>   The day long past we love at last,
> And sigh for that we scorned before."

Or it may be knit to the fourth line:

> She is my store, oh, she my store
> Whose grey eyes wounded me so sore,
>   Who will not place in mine her palm,
> Who will not calm me any more.
>
> (Hyde, *My Love, oh she is my Love*, st. 2.)

These are true units, but they have not the wide
appeal of the simpler units, verse-rimed or cross-rimed.
The enclosed-rimed stanza is rare in Ballad, and is
comparatively rare in Romance:

> 'Twas evening calm, when village maids
>   With Gallia's tuneful sons advance,
>   To frolic in the jovial dance
> 'Mid purple vines and olive shades.
>
> (Landor, *The French Villagers*.)

This form would be little known had it not been made
familiar by Tennyson in his *In Memoriam*; so familiar
that to many it will be a surprise to hear that the
form is uncommon.

Whilst the Romance verse has taken the shape of
many definite stanza-forms, these are neither so varied,
nor so definite in their variation, as the Ballad stanzas,
with the variants Nibelungen and Alexandrine.

The simple Ballad stanza:

> Lo! here the common fault of love,
>   to follow her that flies,
> And fly from her that makes her wail
>   with loud lamenting cries.
>
> (Shakespeare, *Two Gentlemen of Verona*.)

is the form from which spring the whole of the varied
forms of the Ballad stanza, this simple form being the
verse-rimed Ballad-four. It has a sister form, the cross-
rimed Ballad-four, that differs only in the first and third
lines riming as well as the second and fourth:

> Bid me to live, and I will live
>   Thy Protestant to be;
> Or bid me love, and I will give
>   A loving heart to thee.
>   (Herrick, *To Anthea...*, st. 1.)

The first and simplest variant consists of the doubling
of the stanza, making the Ballad-eight; and this may
be verse-rimed, or cross-rimed, or leonine-cross-rimed,
as in the three examples following:

> When chill November's surly blast
>   Made fields and forest bare,
> One ev'ning as I wander'd forth
>   Along the banks of Ayr,
> I spied a man whose aged step
>   Seem'd weary, worn with care,
> His face was furrow'd o'er with years,
>   And hoary was his hair.
>   (Burns, *Man was made to mourn*, st. 1.)

> Robin, thou hast heard sung and say,
>   In gests and storys auld,
> The man that will not when he may
>   Sall have nocht when he wald.
> I pray to heaven baith nicht and day,
>   Be eiked their cares sae cauld,
> That presses first with thee to play
>   By forrest, firth, or fauld.
>   (Henryson, *Robin and Makyne*, st. 12.)

> I make it kend, he that will spend,
>   And luve God late and air,
> He will him mend, and Grace him send,
>   Quhyle catives shall have care:
> And praise weil pend, sall him comend,
>   That of his rowth can spare;
> We knaw the end, that all maun wend
>   Away nakit and bare.
>
> (Blyth, *Advice to be liberal and blyth*, st. 1.)

Even with such full riming the stanza is inclined to break into two units; Henryson's, in fact, is two. That the individuality of the unit appeals to the poet, and appeals to different poets differently when composite units or doublets such as the above are in question, is very evident to any student of poetry. John Armstrong wrote:

> No, Delia, 'tis not thy face,
>   Nor form that I admire,
> Although thy beauty and thy grace
>   Might well awake desire.
>
> Something in ev'ry part of thee
>   To praise, to love, I find,
> But dear as is the form to me,
>   Still dearer is thy mind.

These two stanzas, on Burns giving them a "Scots dress," became a single stanza, a doublet:

> It is na, Jean, thy bonie face
>   Nor shape that I admire,
> Altho' thy beauty and thy grace
>   Might weel awauk desire.
> Something in ilka part o' thee
>   To praise, to love, I find,
> But dear as is thy form to me,
>   Still dearer is thy mind.

Burns's stanza, whilst one thought runs through the

whole, still divides; it is a doublet rather than a single coherent stanza.

Various devices have been adopted for welding the two parts together: the two following are examples:

> My daddie's a delver of dykes,
>   My mither can card and spin,
> And I am a fine fodgel lass,
>   And the siller comes linkin' in:
> The siller comes linkin' in,
>   And it is fu' fair to see,
> And fifty times wow! O wow!
>   What ails the lads at me?
>
> *(Slighted Nancy*, st. 2.)
>
> A wet sheet and a flowing sea,
>   A wind that follows fast,
> And fills the white and rustling sail,
>   And bends the gallant mast:
> And bends the gallant mast, my boys,
>   While, like the eagle free,
> Away the good ship flies, and leaves
>   Old England on the lea.
>
> (Cunningham, *A wet Sheet...*, st. 1.)

Even with the knitting together by repetition such as the above, the eight-lined stanza is inclined to break into two four-lined stanzas; so that whilst there is an undoubted eight-lined unit, it is no more than a doubling of the primal indivisible four-lined unit.

Meineke held that the *Odes* of Horace were to be broken into four-lined stanzas, and many have agreed with him. Professor Postgate, however, discussing the question in 1918, summed up by deciding that "for the great majority of the *Odes* of Horace the four-lined hypothesis is true but devoid of significance." If true, it surely is significant; and the significance is that the law operating in all accentual poetry operated also in Latin poetry, and, considering the lyric origin of the hexameter, in Greek poetry too. As will be seen in the examples occurring later on in this chapter, the short lines in Horace's *Odes* have their counterpart in accentual stanzas; and if in his time the stanza-unit was not so clearly developed as in modern poetry, it is evident that there was the decided trend in the direction of definite form.

It has been noted that the Romance couplet at times augments to a triplet: the Ballad-verse couplet augments in a similar way, producing what has been called a Ballad-six:

> And I would never tire, Janet,
> In fairy-land to dwell;
> But aye at every seven years
> They pay the teind to hell;
> And though the Queen mak's much o' me,
> I fear 'twill be mysell.
>
> (*The Young Tamlane.*)

This form appears very commonly in the old ballads: it is a definite unit, incapable of being split into two smaller complete units, and it was evidently accepted by reciters, and writers, and hearers, as a definite unit. It is at times apparently avoided by repetition:

> O quit thy sword, and bend thy bow,
> And give me kisses three;
> For though I am a poisonous worm,
> No hurt I'll do to thee.
>
> O quit thy sword, and bend thy bow,
> And give me kisses three;
> If I'm not won ere the sun go down,
> Won I shall never be.
>
> (*The Laidly Worm...*, st. 27, 28.)

> King Arthur lives in merry Carlisle,
>   And seemly is to see;
> And there he hath with him Queen Guenever,
>   The bride so bright of blee.
>
> And there he hath with him Queen Guenever,
>   The bride so bright in bower;
> And all his barons about him stoode,
>   That were both stiff and stowre.
>
> <div align="right">(<i>Fragment of the Marriage of Gawaine</i>, st. 1, 2.)</div>

These beautiful repetitions are probably no indication
of any deliberate avoidance of the Ballad-six; but it
is evident how easily a reciter might produce a Ballad-
six by simply dropping the repetition in stanzas such
as the first above quoted. It would be remarkable,
too, if no reciter introduced a change, seemingly
inevitable, into the third line of the second stanza,
making the rime a leonine:

> If I'm not won ere set of sun.

The doubling of the first half of a Ballad verse has
already been spoken of in connection with the breath-
unit:

> Faire Christabelle, that ladye bright,
>   Was had forthe of the towre;
> But ever she droopeth in her minde,
> As nipt by an ungentle winde
>   Doth some faire lillye flowre.
>
> <div align="right">(<i>Sir Cauline</i>, pt. 2, st. 9.)</div>

It is impossible to say what may have been the reason
for this doubling. The verse is the average length of a
sentence; it may be that the composer of the ballad,
on a thought appearing that was too long for an average
verse, doubled the half-verse rather than reduce the

thought. It is evident that he could quite easily have shortened the three lines to two:

> And ever she droopeth in her minde
> As doth some lillye flowre,

but it is as evident that he wished to preserve the full beauty of the thought, and found that the rhythm-sense of his hearers, with his own, readily caught the enlarged metre, as it caught the "My Dear" enlargement. It may be, on the other hand, that he was simply varying the usual metre, and must enlarge the thought to preserve the unit. Yet again, the variation may have been purely instinctive, as the rhythm-sense seems instinctive, the composer himself being quite unable to explain it, even had he been aware of it. There are ten of these augmented stanzas in the ninety-four of *Sir Cauline*; there are three Ballad-sixes.

The first line, instead of the third, is doubled in the following:

> I wandered in a lonely glade,
> Where, issuing from the forest shade,
>   A little mountain stream
> Along the winding valley play'd,
>   Beneath the morning beam.
> (J. Montgomery, A Walk in Spring, st. 1.)

This form, which may be called the Lonely Glade stanza, is less usual, though it has been long in use. In the third of the York Mystery Plays appears the stanza:

> And leyd your lyves in good degre,
> Adam here make I the
>   A man of mykyll myght;
> Thys same shall thy subget be
>   And Eve her name shall hight.

These lines, in an Elizabethan hand, are inserted in the margin of the manuscript to follow line 44. The preceding lines are arranged in four-lined stanzas of eight-syllabled lines cross-rimed.

The form in *Sir Cauline* struck Percy, who in the *Reliques* remarks, "There is something peculiar in the metre of this old ballad: it is not unusual to meet with redundant stanzas of six lines [that is, the ballad-six] but the occasional insertion of a double third or fourth line...is an irregularity I do not remember to have seen elsewhere." The variant as it occurs in *Sir Cauline* may be called the Christabelle stanza.

It is much less usual to find the even lines, the second or fourth, doubled, as in the Fond Lover stanza:

> Why so pale and wan, fond lover?
>   Prithee, why so pale?
> Will, when looking well can't move her,
>   Looking ill prevail?
>   Prithee, why so pale?
>
> (Suckling, *Why so pale...*, st. 1.)

It is probable that the intention was to double the fourth line, though in effect the doubling is really a doubling of the third so far as metre is concerned, the fourth unit being represented by a pause which is perfectly filled in the *My Dear* manner:

> Why so pale and wan, fond lover?
>   Prithee, why so pale?
> Will, when looking well can't move her,
>   Looking ill prevail,
>   Fond lover?
>   Prithee, why so pale?

The second line is doubled in Swinburne's *Neap Tide*. The pause which always follows the first line of the

pair makes it doubtful if the line was intended by the
poet as a doubling of the first line or the second.
There is less doubt as to what the poet intended when
the actual words are repeated:

> In Wakefield there lives a jolly pindèr,
>> In Wakefield all on a green,
>> In Wakefield all on a green:
>
> There is neither knight nor squire, said the pindèr,
>> Nor baron that is so bold,
>> Nor baron that is so bold,
> Dare make a trespàss to the town of Wakefield,
>> But his pledge goes to the pinfold,
>>> etc.
>
>> *(The Jolly Pinder*, opening.)

The etc. no doubt means that the line preceding is to
be repeated in the same manner; but the filling in of
the metre as before:

> In Wakefield all on a green,
>> a green,
> In Wakefield all on a green,

shews that there has been a doubling, and it is perhaps
inessential to consider whether it is the odd line or the
even line that has been doubled.

The doubling of the even lines comes much more
naturally in Romance metre; and whilst the doubling
of the odd line probably originated in Ballad, the
doubling of the even possibly originated in Romance.

The two main forms of this doubling, as seen in the
Christabelle and the Lonely Glade stanzas, are but
intermediaries of a yet more popular form, the
Dowsabel stanza, where both first and third lines are
doubled:

> This maiden in a morne betime
> Went forth, when May was in her prime,
>   To get sweet cetywall,
> The honeysuckle, the harlocke,
> The lilly and the lady-smocke
>   To deck her Summer hall.
>
> (Drayton, *Dowsabel*, st. 6.)

The Ballad-four by this doubling becomes a stanza of six lines, but altogether different in character from the Ballad-six. The latter contains three full verses, taken in three breaths; the former, the Dowsabel stanza, contains two enlarged verses, taken in two breaths. It has long been a popular stanza, and was known as "rime couée," or tail-rime, probably through its sometimes being printed:

> This maiden in a morne betime   } To get sweet cetywall,
> Went forth, when May was in her prime,}
> The honeysuckle, the harlocke,   } To deck her Summer
> The lilly and the lady-smocke   }   hall.

And again:

> Alone walking   }
> In thought plaining } all desolate,
> And sore sighing   }
>
> Me rememb'ring   }
> Of my living   } both early and late.
> My death wishing   }
>
> (Chaucer, *Virelai.*)

where it is seen that the tails rime. There is no doubt here about the bracketed lines being taken in a breath; is it likely that a new breath would be taken for the short tail-line?

Professor Saintsbury considers the term "rime couée" more applicable to verses of the Latin form:

> Pauper amabilis et venerabilis est benedictus,
> Dives inutilis insatiabilis est maledictus.

Such verses, however, internally-rimed, are parallels of quite another metre, the unpaused Alexandrine, or Alexandrin trimetre of Victor Hugo already referred to. The Dowsabel stanza he calls a Romance-six, but it is rather a development from a Ballad-four than from the Romance couplet. Professor Saintsbury thinks it may have developed from the couplet by the addition of a short unrimed line; but with the Christabelle stanza before us, the development by the doubling of the long line seems more likely.

There is yet another way in which the "rime couée" has been printed:

> This maiden in a morne betime Went forth, when May was in
>   her prime,
>   To get sweet cetywall,
> The honeysuckle, the harlocke, The lilly and the lady-smocke
>   To deck her Summer hall.

It is quite evident that these forms are but writers' or printers' devices; the stanza would hardly take definite shape in the mind when heard, any more than a melody takes a shape. Certain repetitions are noted, phrases in music, rimes in poetry. It is possible that the hearers were conscious but of a long couplet, clinched by the rime; and that the Dowsabel stanza was thought a long couplet is shewn in *A Nest of Ninnies*, 1608, by Robert Armin, where the following occurs:

"...The king, the jester, and all gathers about him to see him eate it. Will begins thus to rime over his milk:

> This bit, Harry, I give to thee, and this next bit must serve
>   for me, both which Ile eat apace;
> This, madam, unto you, and this bit I myself eate now, and all
>   the rest upon thy face,

meaning the foole, in whose beard and head the bread
and milk were thick sowne, and his eyes almost put
out...."

This is a Dowsabel stanza, with the last verse full
Romance instead of Ballad:

> This bit, Harry, I give to thee,
> And this next bit must serve for me,
>   Both which Ile eat apace;
> This, madam, unto you,
> And this bit I myself eate now,
>   And all the rest upon thy face.

Schipper suggests that the short lines were originally
refrains following Romance couplets, an origin akin to
that suggested by Professor Saintsbury; but in most
instances, as in the above, the thought occupies the
entire length of the three lines.

As the Ballad-eight, or the Ballad-six may be on
two rimes, so may the Dowsabel stanza; or the two
halves may be musically knit together as in E. B.
Browning's *A Sabbath Morning at Sea* (st. 6):

> I oft had seen the dawnlight run
>   As red wine, through the hills, and break
>   Through many a mist's inurning;
> But here, no earth profaned the sun!
>   Heaven, ocean, did alone partake
>   The sacrament of morning.

This stanza shews clearly, too, how it is composed of
two long verses.

As the Ballad-four may be augmented in either
verse by the Christabelle doubling, so too may the
Ballad-six: the doubling may be in one, two, or three
verses. As, too, the Ballad-six may appear in the midst
of Ballad-fours, so amongst what may be called Dowsabel-fours appear Dowsabel-sixes. The ballad *The*

Felon Sow of Rokeby is in Dowsabel-fours, and one stanza among the forty that compose the ballad is a Dowsabel-six, that is, a Ballad-six where the first, third, and fifth lines have been doubled.

The following stanza from *All's Well that Ends Well* shews clearly how the lines are a doubling, and shews the Ballad-eight composed of Ballad-four and Dowsabel-four:

> Was this fair face the cause, quoth she,
>> Why the Grecians sackèd Troy?
> Fond done, done fond,
>> Was this king Priam's joy?
> With that she sighèd as she stood,
> With that she sighèd as she stood,
>> And gave this sentence then;
> Among nine bad if one be good,
> Among nine bad if one be good,
>> There's yet one good in ten.

The Dowsabel-eight is the stanza used by Chaucer in *The Tale of Sir Thopas*. The printed poem is not divided into stanzas, but splits up naturally with almost perfect regularity.

If, for purposes of stanza-variation, or for thought-accommodation, or for any purpose whatsoever, a Christabelle or Dowsabel doubling could take place, there need be nothing to prevent a trebling; and the trebling occurs from very early times, as in what may be called the Sweet May stanza:

> Ase y me rod this ender day,
> By grene wode to seche play,
> Mid herte y thohte al on a may,
>> Suetest of alle thinge;
> Luthe, and ich on telle may
>> Al of that suete thinge.

The third line is trebled in Kipling's *The Last Suttee*, and the trebled line also occurs in No. 9 of the York Plays. When both first and third are trebled the popular Nymphidia stanza results:

> Old Chaucer doth of Topas tell,
> Mad Rabelais of Pantagruel,
> A later third of Dowsabel
>   With such like trifles playing;
> Others the like have laboured at,
> Some of this thing and some of that,
> And many of that they know not what,
>   But that they must be saying.
>
> (Drayton, Nymphidia, st. 1.)

As in the song from *All's Well that Ends Well*, examples occur where the words themselves are repeated:

> Saw ye na my Peggy,
> Saw ye na my Peggy,
> Saw ye na my Peggy,
>   Coming o'er the lea?
> Sure a finer creature
> Ne'er was form'd by nature,
> So complete each feature,
>   So divine is she.
>
> (Burns, Saw ye na…, st. 1.)

In Kipling's *The Young British Soldier*, the third line is repeated in this way, and in a drinking-song *Bacchus' Health*, the first and third are repeated.

The Ballad-six and the Ballad-eight follow the Ballad-four in trebling, an excellent example where the fifth and seventh lines are trebled being the well-known **King Cophetua and the Beggar Maid**. An example of this vigorous King Cophetua stanza is quoted (st. 2):

The blinded boy, that shoots so trim,
 From heaven downe did hie;
He drew a dart and shot at him,
 In place where he did lye;
Which soon did pierse him to the quicke,
And when he felt the arrow pricke,
Which in his tender heart did sticke,
 He looketh as he would dye.
"What sudden chance is this," quoth he,
"That I to love must subject be,
Which never thereto would agree,
 But still did it defie?"

Schipper perceived that this trebled form was a development of the doubled form, but apparently did not see that the latter might in like manner be a development of the ordinary stanza. He failed, moreover, to perceive that the stanza:

Thir ladyis fair,
That makis repair,
And in the court ar kend,
Thre dayis thair
They will do mair,
Ane mater for till end,
Than thair guid men
Will do in ten,
For ony craft they can;
So weill they ken
Quhat tyme and quhen
Thair menes thay sowld mak then.
   (Dunbar, *Of the Ladyis...*

is not a species of "tail-rhyme" similar to the Dowsabel stanza. And he failed because he failed in the first place to perceive the natural verse-unit; for he says, "With regard to the limit of the number of feet permissible

A   10

in a line or verse, no fixed rule can be laid down." The
above is no more than a Ballad-eight with leonine rime:

> Thir ladyis fair, that makis repair,
>   And in the court ar kend,
> Thre dayis thair thay will do mair,
>   Ane mater for till end,...

The classic form of the trebled verse is the Kirkconnell stanza:

> I wish I were where Helen lies;
> Night and day on me she cries;
> O that I were where Helen lies
>   On fair Kirkconnell lea.
>
> Curst be the heart that thought the thought,
> And curst the hand that fired the shot
> When in my arms burd Helen dropt,
>   And died to succour me.
>
> *(Helen of Kirkconnell*, st. 1 and 2.)

The rime of the short lines knits these two amplified
verses into one stanza; but the short lines rime throughout the ballad, so it is printed in four-lined stanzas.
Even when clearly bound by the rime the stanza may
be and often is printed in this broken form, as in
Stevenson's *Requiem.* This was first written in three
stanzas; an amplified Ballad-six.

It cannot be stated definitely how far the verse-
unit, as consonant with the breath-unit, may be carried
in the matter of amplifying. It is, however, almost
certain that, as the ordinary Ballad verse is taken in a
breath, so the Christabelle verse will be taken in a
breath; that is, the full stanza in two breaths. The
construction may, and often does, give opportunity for
breath at the end of the first line of the doubled line,
but the whole is usually so knit that the oneness of

the thought causes the whole to be taken in one breath instinctively, and without difficulty. The Nymphidia and Kirkconnell stanzas may possibly require, at any rate they will allow, two breaths for each amplified verse; for be it noted, the trebling brings the verse back to two averages, and the stanza will probably be read with a quick breath after the second line, the equivalent of the Romance couplet, and a leisurely breath after the Ballad verse following. It is, however, quite possible, and is not difficult, to speak the whole in one breath.

There are few examples of the line being quadrupled. Longfellow has one, *The Goblet of Life*; and Swinburne has one, *A Child's Laughter*. A good example occurs in the second half of the Jockey to the Fair stanza; and as the naturalness of a stanza is largely attested by its popularity, one from the song *With Jockey to the Fair* (st. 5) is quoted:

> Soon did they meet a joyful throng,
> Their gay companions blithe and young;
> Each joins the dance, each joins the song,
>   To hail the happy pair.
> What two were e'er so fond as they?
> All bless the kind propitious day,
> The smiling morn, and blooming May,
> When lovely Jenny ran away
>   With Jockey to the Fair.

Though this metre is felt to be natural, it is evidently the extreme of the augmented forms, for there are few examples of it. It would almost appear as though too frequent riming on one sound causes the lyric bond of such stanzas to be obscured or lost; the lines become

rather "batches" or "tirades" of Romance lines. The
effect is similar to the quadrupling when the four lines
are in two couplets:

> In death-sheets lieth Rosalind,
> > As white and still as they;
> And the old nurse that watched her bed,
> > Rose up with "Well-a-day!"
> And opened the casement to let in
> The sun, and that sweet doubtful din
> Which droppeth from the grass and bough
> Sans wind and bird—none knoweth how—
> > To cheer her as she lay.
>
> > (E. B. Browning, *The Poet's Vow*, pt. 4, st. 1.)

This poem shews excellently the varied swelling of
the Ballad verse, and the same is shewn in a poem of
five stanzas by Poe:

> The ring is on my hand,
> > And the wreath is on my brow;
> Satins and jewels grand
> Are all at my command,
> > And I am happy now.
>
> And my lord he loves me well;
> > But, when first he breathed his vow,
> I felt my bosom swell—
> For the words sang as a knell
> And the voice seemed *his* who fell
> In the battle down the dell,
> > And who is happy now.
>
> > .   .   .   .   .   .
>
> And thus the words were spoken,
> > And thus the plighted vow;
> And though my faith be broken,
> And though my heart be broken,
> Behold the golden token
> > That *proves* me happy now.
>
> > (Poe, *Bridal Ballad*, st. 1, 2, and 4.)

In the following examples, two cross-rimed stanzas
have been knit into one as if they were instances of
quadrupling; and the result, especially in the second,
which has the Ballad termination, is much more pleasing
than the actually quadrupled verses:

> My mother's grave, my mother's grave!
>   Oh! dreamless is her slumber there,
> And drowsily the banners wave
>   O'er her that was so chaste and fair;
>   Yea! love is dead, and memory faded!
> But when the dew is on the brake,
>   And silence sleeps o'er earth and sea,
> And mourners weep, and ghosts awake,
>   Oh! then she cometh back to me,
>   In her cold beauty darkly shaded!
>   (Praed, *Songs from The Troubadour*, No. 1, st. 1.)

> O love! O beauteous Love!
>   Thy home is made for all sweet things,
> A dwelling for thine own soft dove
>   And souls as spotless as her wings;
>   There summer ceases never:
> The trees are rich with luscious fruits,
>   The bowers are full of joyous throngs,
> And gales that come from Heaven's own lutes
>   And rivulets whose streams are songs
>   Go murmuring on for ever!
>   (Praed, *Song*, st. 1.)

The foregoing examples shew verse-units, or breath-
units, longer than the average: a few of the many that
occur shorter than the average have been quoted in
Chapter III.

The shortening of the even lines of the stanza
may occur even where the verse has first been
amplified:

I never shall love the snow again
   Since Maurice died:
With corniced drifts it blocked the lane
And sheeted in a desolate plain
   The country side.

(Bridges, No. 11, Book 5, st. 1.)

Sweet Sussex owl, so trimly dight
With feathers, like a lady bright,
Thou sing'st alone, sitting by night,
   Te whit, te whoo!
Thy note that forth so freely rolls,
With shrill command the mouse controls,
And sings a dirge for dying souls,
   Te whit, te whoo!

(Vautor, *Sweet Sussex Owl*.)

A wayle whyt as whalles bon,
A grain in golde that goldly shon,
A tortle that min herte is on,
   In townes trewe,
Hire gladshipe nes never gon,
   Whil y may glewe.

(Song from Harleian MS. 2253.)

The last shews how the first verse, trebled in its first
half, reduced in its second, and the second verse normal
in its first half and reduced in its second, results in the
famous Burns stanza. It was at one time extremely
popular. It is used extensively in the "York Mystery
Plays," forming the metre of four entire plays, variations
of it being used in others. These plays were composed
about 1340—1350. In Play 6 the first line has in four
stanzas been doubled only instead of trebled, and the
modern editor of the plays notes "a line seems wanting
here": but it is evident that the poet, or the scribe, or
both, felt, as Schipper felt in modern times, that the
stanza with the line doubled was the equivalent of the
one with the line trebled.

If a line may shorten till only one unit remains, is it possible that a line may be dropped altogether? This may be difficult to prove; but if the music of three silent units can be heard, as it is when the line contains one unit only, may it not be possible for the first half of the verse to suggest the second half though that be quite absent? Take, for example, Shakespeare's song, so well wedded to music by Schubert,—"Who is Silvia":—take especially the third stanza:

> Then to Silvia let us sing,
>   That Silvia is excelling;
> She excels each mortal thing
>   Upon the dull earth dwelling;
> To her let us garlands bring.

Here, as in the second stanza, the thought is rounded off at the end of the fourth line; each verse is a complete thought, and the semi-isolation of the last line breeds in the mind a strain of complementary music—a short line rhyming with "dwelling,"

> To her let us garlands bring,
>   Our adoration telling,

or as it might be. Even if no words flow with it in the imagination,—and no words are necessary,—the inner-sounding music of such a close is charming; its absence takes nothing from an exquisite stanza, whilst its presence in the imagination adds an indefinable sweetness. There is no least suggestion that this Silvia stanza ought to contain six lines;—the suggestion is simply that a verse may shorten by dropping the entire second half. If the poet is able to use more or less of the norm to produce a fine stanza, well; the lyric is the end, the norm only the means. Christina Rossetti uses the full norm of Shakespeare's stanza, varying the initial units of the odd lines:

> The year stood at the equinox
>   And bluff the north was blowing,
> A bleat of lambs came from the flocks,
>   Green hardy things were growing;
> I met a maid with shining locks
>   Where milky kine were lowing.
>
> (*A Farm Walk*, st. 1.)

The closing music suggested in Shakespeare's stanza is yet more definitely awakened in the following, where the third line has been trebled, and its second half dropped:

> Yet my feet liked the dances well,
>   The songs went to my voice,
> The music made me shake and weep;
> And often, all night long, my sleep
> Gave dreams I had been fain to keep.
>
> (D. G. Rossetti, *The Bride's Dream*, st. 41.)

With the full stop omitted, an unheard melody continues, the words floating upon it, being a suggestion of "My heart did so rejoice."

Again, there is no suggestion that the short line should follow the trebled line; it is sought only to discover what stanza-norms there may be, and to see how cunningly the poets vary the norms, neither forsaking them, nor breaking them.

That there is a shortening of the first line possible is evident, since a shortening of the first half of a Ballad verse results in a Nibelungen verse, a further shortening in an Alexandrine. This shortening may take place in a line that has first been doubled:

> Saw ye the blazing star?
> The heavens looked down on freedom's war
>   And lit her torch on high!
> Bright on her dragon crest
> It tells that glory's wings shall rest,
>   When warriors meet to die!
>
> (Hemans, *Owen Glyndwr's War-Song*, st. 1.)

In lines one and four, as in three and six, there is the palpable pause indicating a dropped unit: this pause clearly makes a Dowsabel stanza of the above:

> Saw ye (above) the blazing star?
> The heavens looked down on freedom's war
>   And lit her torch on high!
> Bright on her (lifted) dragon crest
> It tells that glory's wings shall rest,
>   Where warriors meet to die!

A shortening of a similar kind occurs in another of Mrs Hemans's lyrics:

> A voice from Scio's isle—
> A voice of song, a voice of old,
> Swept far as cloud on billow rolled,
>   And earth was hushed the while—
>
> (Hemans, *The Voice of Scio*, st. 1.)

Here the rime connects lines one and four instead of one and two, and lines two and three rime together, making the stanza a ballad variant of the *In Memoriam* stanza. It is as though the halves of the first verse had been transposed, as is evident when the stanza is printed:

> A voice of song, a voice of old,
>   A voice from Scio's isle,
> Swept far as cloud on billow rolled,
>   And earth was hushed the while.

The pause after the short line of Mrs Hemans's stanza isolates it, whilst the last three are perfectly knit. Is it possible that the line is the result of dropping the first half of a verse, and that the Scio's Isle stanza is a broken Christabelle stanza? For example:

> (The listeners on the verges heard)
>   A voice from Scio's isle—
> A voice of song, a voice of old,
> Swept far as cloud on billow rolled,
>   And earth was hushed the while—

This appears plausible; but it is not probable. The imagination readily completes the music of a broken verse if the opening be given; and on the short-line opening being heard, the imagination immediately expects an Alexandrine, and is at first baffled by the line of four units following; anticipation is disappointed. Now the very charm of the various rhythms is that they may be anticipated;—the poet must be in league with his hearers, must avoid disappointing them;—that is, if he is to please any one but himself. Hearing the conclusion of the above stanza, the impression left is that of a broken Christabelle or Kirkconnell stanza:

> A voice from Scio's isle ('tis told),
> A voice of song, a voice of old,
> Swept far as cloud on billow rolled,
>   And earth was hushed the while.

Again, the proof that a doubtful norm such as the above is unacceptable, both to poet and to hearer, is the fact that the form has so seldom been used;—the clear-cut forms abound by the hundred thousand, in all tongues;—their music, too, is independent of speech, and is understood wherever the heart pulses, and the breath trembles.

The form is cross-rimed in the following:

> The dew no more will weep
> The primrose's pale cheek to deck;
> The dew no more will sleep
> Nuzzel'd in the lily's neck;
> Much rather would it be thy tear,
> And leave them both to tremble here.
>
> (Crashaw, *Saint Mary Magdalene*, st. 7.)

Here the verses palpably are Romance verses, a unit having been dropped from the first line of the couplet.

A striking illustration of the way in which the shortening may come about is the following:

> Autumn and Winter,
> Summer and Spring—
> Hath time no other song to sing?
> Weary we grow of the changeless tune—
> June and December,
> December and June!
>> (Le Gallienne, *Time's Monotone*, st. 1.)

Drop the first and fifth lines, and the result is:

> Summer and Spring—
> Hath time no other song to sing?
> Weary we grow of the changeless tune—
> December and June!

It is evident that the first three lines of the stanza are one verse, the second three one:

> Autumn and Winter, Summer and Spring—
> Hath time no other song to sing?

so that the shortening results from dropping half of a Romance line.

The norms are perfect even when broken, so long as they clearly reveal, in their music, their connection with the basic norm. If they vary too much, their appeal is restricted.

Verses of Romance metre are subject to the same amplifying as Ballad. The second or fourth line shortened would of course result in Ballad and its variants. The Romance doublings are not, however, so spontaneous as those in the Ballad metre, where the pause at the end of the verse seems to give spring to the opening of the verse following.

The doubling of the even lines is more evident in the Romance:

> You meaner beauties of the night,
>   That poorly satisfie our eies
> More by your number than your light,
>   You common people of the skies,
>   What are you when the moon shall rise?
> (Wotton, On his Mistress..., st. 1.)

Owing to the absence of the pause, too, the verse-units are more inclined to be obscured by the overflowing of the sentence from verse to verse. The obscuring of the form is particularly shewn in stanzas such as:

> So let me lie, and, calm as they,
> Let beam upon my inward view
> Those eyes of deep, soft lucent hue—
> Eyes too expressive to be blue,
> Too lovely to be grey.
> (M. Arnold, On the Rhine, st. 4.)

The thought evidently breaks at 'hue,' but the rime 'blue' connects it up again, and the sense of harmony is not satisfied. Satisfaction comes with a slight alteration:

> So let me lie, and, calm as they,
>   Let beam upon my inward view
>   Those eyes of deep, soft lucent hue—
> Eyes too expressive to be grey,
>   Too lovely to be blue.

The stanza now appears more rounded, more balanced; it closes with a ballad verse, and the enclosed couplet appears as a doubled second line. Did the thought overrun from the third line to the fourth, however, then it would be felt that the last line, the short one, should be dropped, an *In Memoriam* stanza resulting:

> So let me lie, and, calm as they,
> > Let beam upon my inward view
> > Those eyes, too lovely to be blue
> And too expressive to be grey.

No alteration is suggested; it is not suggested that the stanza *should* be other than it is.

Coleridge's alteration of a stanza in *The Ancient Mariner* may be quoted to shew the instinctive feeling of the poet as to the identity of the Romance verse, the Ballad verse, and the amplified verse. In the 1798 edition of the poem there is a single Romance stanza:

> Are those her naked ribs, which fleck'd
> > The sun that did behind them peer?
> And are those two all, all her crew,
> > That woman and her fleshless Pheere?

This stanza was in 1800 altered to:

> Are those her ribs through which the sun
> > Did peer as through a grate?
> And is that woman all her crew?
> Is that a Death? and are there two?
> > Is Death that woman's mate? (part 3, st. 10.)

It might be supposed that with so much variation by doubling, trebling, and quadrupling, shortening one or more lines, the average verse would be smothered and lost. It will be found, however, that the average, the norm, is never lost; that the number of variations, whilst very great, is nevertheless limited, and that out of a very great number possible only a very few, comparatively, have become fixed as permanent variations.

Very few Romance stanzas need be quoted to shew the doubling, trebling and quadrupling, parallel to that which takes place in Ballad stanzas:

> All through the sultry hours of June,
> From morning blithe to golden noon,
> 　And till the star of evening climbs
> The gray-blue East, a world too soon,
> 　　There sings a thrush amid the limes.
>
> 　　　　　　(Collins, *My Thrush*, st. 1.)

> Hearing that Chloe's bower crown'd
> 　The summit of a neighbouring hill,
> Where every rural joy was found,
> Where health and wealth were plac'd around,
> 　To wait like servants on her will.
>
> 　　　　　(Rowe, *Occasioned by...Lady Warwick*, st. 1.)

> O thou whose happy pencil strays
> Where I am call'd nor dare to gaze,
> 　But lower my eye and check my tongue;
> O, if thou valuest peaceful days,
> Pursue the ringlet's sunny maze,
> 　And dwell not on those lips too long.
>
> 　　　　　　(Landor, No. 6 of *Selections.*)

> Here's merry Christmas come again,
> 　With all it ever used to bring;
> The mistletoe and carol strain,
> The holly in the window pane,
> And all the bloom from hill and plain
> 　The winter's chilly hand can fling.
>
> 　　　　　(E. Cook, *Here's merry Christmas...*, st. 1.)

> O were I able to rehearse
> My ewie's praise in proper verse,
> I'd sound it out as loud and fierce
> 　As ever piper's drone could blaw,
> My ewie with the crooked horn
> Weel deserved baith garse and corn;
> Sic a ewie ne'er was born
> 　Here abouts nor far awa.
>
> 　　　　　(Skinner, *The Ewie wi' the crooked Horn*, st. 1.)

The day her builders made their halt,
Those cities of the lake of salt
Stood firmly 'stablished without·fault,
Made proud with pillars of basalt,
  With sardonyx and porphyry.
The day that Jonah bore abroad
To Nineveh the voice of God,
A brackish lake lay in his road,
Where erst Pride fixed her sure abode,
  As then in royal Nineveh.
          (D. G. Rossetti, *The Burden of Nineveh*, st. 13.)

If the dread day that calls thee hence,
  Through a red mist of fear should loom,
  (Closing in deadliest night and gloom
Long aching hours of dumb suspense,)
  And leave me to my lonely doom.
                    (Procter, *Life in Death*..., st. 1.)

You meaner beauties of the night,
  That poorly satisfie our eies
More by your number than your light,
  You common people of the skies,
  What are you when the moon shall rise?
                    (Wotton, *On his Mistress*..., st. 1.)

I climbed the stair in Antwerp church,
  What time the circling thews of sound
  At sunset seemed to heave it round.
Far up, the carillon did search
The wind, and the birds came to perch
  Far under, where the gables wound.
          (D. G. Rossetti, *Antwerp and Bruges*, st. 1.)

Let not woman e'er complain
  Of inconstancy in love;
Let not woman e'er complain
  Fickle man is apt to rove;
Look abroad through Nature's range,
Nature's mighty law is change;
Ladies, would it not be strange
  Man should then a monster prove?
                (Burns, *Let not woman e'er complain*, st. 1.)

Again, the close connection felt to exist between the Romance and Ballad forms is curiously shewn in Burns's *Scots wha hae*. When he sent the song to G. Thomson for inclusion in his collection of Scottish Airs, Thomson objected to the tune proposed by Burns, *Hey tuttie, taitie*, and proposed as more worthy *Lewie Gordon*. In order to go with this tune, however, the fourth line would require to be lengthened, and he suggested the addition of the words in brackets:

> Scots, wha hae wi' Wallace bled,
> Scots, wham Bruce has aften led,
> Welcome to your gory bed,
> 　Or to (glorious) victorie!
>
> Now's the day, and now's the hour ;—
> See the front o' battle lower;
> See approach proud Edward's power—
> 　(Chains—) chains and slaverie!
>
> Wha will be a traitor-knave?
> Wha can fill a coward's grave?
> Wha sae base as be a slave?
> 　Let him (let him) turn and flee.

Burns agreed to the substitution of the tune, and agreed to the lengthening of the lines, but he did not adopt the suggested amendments, making the end line of the second stanza "Edward! chains and slaverie!" and the end line of the third "Traitor! coward! turn and flee!" etc. The alteration was made known in Currie's *Works*, 1800; Currie demanded that the words as Burns first wrote them, to the tune suggested by him, should be printed, and in 1801 Thomson complied, printing the original words to the tune *Hey tuttie, taitie*,—the tune to which, with slight modifications, the song is now sung. It is strange, though, that Burns, who is said to have thought the ballad *Helen of Kirkconnell* "silly to contemptibility," should have adopted the trochaic form of the Kirkconnell stanza for his ode.

When the even lines are reduced by one unit, they of course become Ballad, and any further reduction is a reduction of the Ballad-verse. One example where the reduction is among Romance verses may be quoted:

> O thou, the wonder of all dayes!
> O Paragon, the Pearle of praise!
> O virgin martyr, ever blest
>   Above the rest
> Of all thy Maiden-Traine! we come
> And bring fresh strewings for thy Tombe.
>   (Herrick, *The Dirge of Jephtha's Daughter*, st. 1.)

A reduction of this kind is avoided by repetition throughout the song in Burns's "O wert thou in the cauld Blast," and Shelley so repeats the phrase of two units in the last line of the following:

> When passion's trance is overpast,
> If tenderness and truth could last
> Or live, whilst all wild feelings keep
> Some mortal slumber, dark and deep,
> I should not weep, I should not weep.
>   (Shelley, *To...*, st. 1.)

The stanza of six lines, four cross-rimed and a closing couplet, has a greater sense of completeness than the parallel Ballad-form:

> My minde to me a kingdom is;
>   Such perfect joy therein I finde
> As farre exceeds all earthly blisse,
>   That God or Nature hath assignde:
> Though much I want, that most would have,
> Yet still my minde forbids to crave.
>   (Dyer, *My minde to me...*, st. 1.)

A

In the Ballad form, where lines two and four are a unit short of the Romance measure, there appears to be a call for a similar short line for the rounding off of the form. This does not mean there is a necessity for such a line, and many readers, perhaps most, would not feel the call of it; but that some do feel the call is evident when it is seen that such stanzas exist. For instance, had the above been written:

> My minde to me a kingdom is;
>   Such joy therein I finde
> As farre exceeds all earthly blisse,
>   That Nature hath assignde:
> Though much I want, that most would have,
> Yet still my minde forbids to crave,—
>   (A kingdom is my minde.)

The stanza appears to give more satisfaction with a final short line, as above, than without it. Again, it is not suggested that the short line ought to be there.

Romance stanzas of eight lines vary in the same way that Ballad stanzas vary. In stanzas of more than eight lines confusion of riming begins to appear, and the stanzas lose definiteness:—actually, they are comparatively small in number, and undistinguished in character. As in Ballad, the smallest definite Romance stanza-unit consists of four lines—two verses—or their equivalent, and the largest of eight lines—four verses;—the lines in most cases may be doubled, trebled, quadrupled, or shortened, as in the examples quoted, and in other definite ways. The tendency towards variations, many of which are now fixed, many abandoned, may be seen in such collections as the York Plays, the Coventry Plays, and the like.

The perfect blending of verses and lines of different lengths depends upon their being perfect wholes or parts of the normal verse-unit. The four main types of lyric verse,—Romance, Ballad, and the two subvarieties of the Ballad, Nibelungen and Alexandrine,—are constantly blended, a fact evident on almost every page of poetry. A most perfect blend of this kind is the following:

> The cold earth slept below,
>   Above, the cold sky shone;
> And all around, with a chilling sound,
>   From caves of ice and fields of snow,
>   The breath of night like death did flow
>   Beneath the sinking moon.

The first verse is Alexandrine, the second Romance, the third Ballad, and the three are closely knit with interwoven rime. The play of pause in the Alexandrine, and filling in the Romance, has great effect; through the pauses the imagination feels the flow of the metre, and the filling comes as agreeable confirmation of the metre imagined. It is this play that is part of the spirit of Macaulay's *Horatius*. The popularity of such poems is largely due to the form in which they are cast; the ebb and flow of the verses respond directly and immediately to the ebb and flow of emotion.

The pause followed by filling causes a great lyric lift, and is of immense influence. This is shewn by the popularity of the *My Dear* filling already noticed, by the equally great popularity of the poulter's measure, and by the slightly varied poulter's measure in which the popular limerick is written. A widely-known example of the mental filling of pauses is the song *John Brown's body lies a-mouldering in the grave*, where word after word is dropped as the song proceeds, until

nothing but the first word 'John' is audible, the rest
being sung in the imagination in the manner too well
known to need description.

Besides combining amongst themselves, the four
Lyric metres also combine, though less spontaneously,
with Heroic, giving rise to a few well-known stanza-
forms. Such combinations usually give more stately
music, the hurry of the Lyric being checked by the
greater deliberateness of the Heroic, but the Heroic
itself being somewhat accelerated by the vivacity of
the Lyric. The stanzas coming from this union form
the basis of the organ-music in British poetry. The most
spontaneous combination is that of the Alexandrine
with the Heroic,—the resulting music being a complete
contrast to the almost frivolous facility of the combined
Alexandrine and Ballad. Perfection is attained in the
canzone form, as illustrated in Hunt's *O Lovely Age of
Gold!* Hunt's translation is much superior, both as a
British stanza-form and as a poem, to the version
purporting to be original, in Daniel's *Delia*. Though
Daniel follows the rime-scheme of the original, with
customary substitution of single for double rimes,
Hunt's rime-scheme is more in accord with British
wont, and the result appeals as more musical and
freely-flowing. In the best examples of the canzone
rhythm, the Alexandrines that alternate with Heroic
verses are in couplets, like the native forms of poulter's
measure and limerick. The final undivided Alexandrine
gives the full stately close to the stanza, as to ordinary
Heroic stanzas such as the Spenserian. It is to be
remarked that the Alexandrine, when used as a couplet,
partakes of lyric vivacity; when written as an undivided

verse, of heroic deliberateness. The fillip seems to be
given by the mid-rime that makes the couplet division.

The normal form of this composite stanza is as under:

> O sister meek of Truth,
> To my admiring youth
> Thy sober air and native charms infuse!
> The flowers that sweetest breathe,
> Though Beauty culled the wreath,
> Still ask thy hand to range their ordered hues.
>
> (Collins, *Ode to Simplicity*, st. 5.)

This form, with the addition of a Romance half-verse
and an undivided Alexandrine, makes the glorious
stanza of Milton's *Hymn*:

> No war, or battle's sound,
> Was heard, the world around;
> The idle spear and shield were high up hung;
> The hooked chariot stood
> Unstained with hostile blood;
> The trumpet spake not to the armed throng;
> And kings sat still, with awful eye,
> As if they surely knew their sovereign Lord was by.
>
> (Milton, *On the Morning of Christ's Nativity*, st. 4.)

One reason, not necessarily the only reason, why
the stanza is of the type shewn in Collins's *Ode*, has
been discussed when dealing with four-syllabled units.
Were the alternate stresses made lighter, both Alexandrines and Heroics would disappear:

> O sìster of the Trùth,
> To mè as to a yòuth
> The sòberness thy nàtive chàrms infùse!
> The flòwers that to me brèathe,
> Though Bèauty cùlled the wrèath,
> Still àsk of thèe to rànge their màny hùes.

The alternate stresses are now subdued, and a subdued stress passes in the pause after every line; and the two halves of the stanza are no longer of irregular lyric construction, since the two lines that formed the Alexandrine have now but four stresses, and the Heroic verse has three, so that a Ballad-verse in four-syllabled rhythm results, and the irregular stanza has become a regular lyric stanza of the simplest kind,—composed, that is, of two Ballad verses.

In the stanzas considered so far rime has shewn itself as a welder of verses into stanzas, and this, with the marking of the verse-ends, was evidently its original function,—apart, that is, from any aesthetic characteristics. Once the stanza forms were established, however, rime assumed a new and apparently contradictory function; it became a disintegrator of stanzas. The disintegration is, however, more apparent to the eye than to the ear; it is rather formal than actual.

Since to the listeners the end of a verse, or of a pair of verses, was accentuated by the rime, so to the writers or readers of printed poetry, the rime became an indication of a line-end, and in writing or printing, the verse was broken into a greater or less number of lines. This breaking took place naturally in the Romance metre, as its evolution was to the couplet form; but in Ballad metre it was by no means invariable, though it was no doubt hastened when mid-rime came into use, making a cross-rimed ballad-four out of a ballad couplet. In accordance as the synonymity of rime and line-end was felt more or less powerfully, so the verses became more or less broken. This, of course, could be so only to readers or writers;—listeners would still hear

the verse as a full unit of thought, hearing the contained
rime-music, but without thinking of the verse broken up
into small portions, except in so far that they would note
that, as the rimes of the full verses marked complete
thoughts, so the contained rimes marked clauses of the
thought.

In the MS. of the Coventry Mystery Plays, the
transcriber found it advisable to do for the eye what the
rime itself did for the ear,—indicate the lines that rimed:

> Allemyghtfful fadyr, mercyful kynge!
> Receyvyth now this lytyl offrynge,
>   ffor it is the first in degré,
> That your lytyl childe so yynge,
> Presentyth today be my shewyng,
>   to your hyg magesté.
> Of his sympyl poverté,
>   Be his devocion and my good wylle;
> Upon your awtere receyve of me,
>   Your sonys offrynge, as it is skylle!

In indentation, the mechanical method of indicating
the riming lines in modern times, the openings of the
riming lines start on the same perpendicular:

> Swallow, my sister, O sister swallow,
>   How can thine heart be full of the Spring?
>   A thousand summers are over and dead.
> What hast thou found in the spring to follow?
>   What hast thou found in thy heart to sing?
>   What wilt thou do when the summer is shed?
>   (Swinburne, *Itylus*, st. 1.)

> And in air the clamorous birds,
>   And men upon earth that hear
> Sweet articulate words
>   Sweetly divided apart,
>   And in shallow and channel and mere
> The rapid and footless herds,
>   Rejoiced, being foolish of heart.
>   (Swinburne, from Chorus in *Atalanta*....

This indenting is not necessary; it was almost entirely ignored by Wordsworth; it was freely and delightfully used by Herrick; it was misused by Southey, or used for another purpose in his arabesques *Thalaba* and *Kehama*. To the writer, indenting has a great charm; it at once gives a cue for the rime-scheme, and pleases the eye as the fall of the rime pleases the ear.

In both Ballad and Romance it is clearly seen how the full verses naturally break into even parts. In both, the full verses of eight units are knit first into long couplets:

Ye banks and braes o' bonie Doon, how can ye bloom sae fresh and fair?
How can ye chant, ye little birds, and I sae weary, fu' o' care?

and

Sweet are the banks, the banks of Doon, the spreading flowers are fair,
And everything is blythe, and glad, but I am fu' o' care.

There is no cross-riming, though each verse naturally breaks into two lines of even length, the sentence consisting of two clauses. In the same way the clauses, more especially the one in the first half of the verse, often divide into two equal sub-clauses:

Sweet are the banks,	the banks of Doon.
How can ye chant,	ye little birds.
Thou'll break my heart,	thou warbling bird.

As at the verse-end rime appears and knits the verses into long couplets, or short ones, or into cross-rimed stanzas according to which ends rime, so the smaller breaks are inclined to be knit into couplets with internal rime, this riming of half-lines being called leonine:

Biancha, let me pay the debt
  I owe thee for a kiss
Thou lent'st to me; and I to thee
  Will render ten for this.
           (Herrick, *Kissing Usurie*, st. 1.)

Guest remarks, "when, as is sometimes the case, the middle rime occurs regularly, it would perhaps be better to divide the line." This Coleridge did not do, but Herrick did, printing the above stanza:

> Biancha, let
> Me pay the debt
> I owe thee for a kiss
> Thou lent'st to me;
> And I to thee
> Will render ten for this.

Further, the half-stanza:

> Melt, melt my pains,
> With thy soft strains;
> That having ease me given,
> With full delight,
> I leave this light;
> And take my flight
> For Heaven.

> (Herrick, *To music*..., part st. 3.)

The verse-units, and the stanza-units, are the same however they may be printed. What Shakespeare prints in the following way:

> The raging rocks
> And shivering shocks
> Shall break the locks
> Of prison gates;
> And Phibbus' car
> Shall shine from far,
> And make and mar
> The foolish fates.

> (*Midsummer-Night's Dream*, 1, 2.)

another may print:

> The raging rocks and shivering shocks
> Shall break the locks of prison gates;
> And Phibbus' car shall shine from far,
> And make and mar the foolish fates.

And another:

> The raging rocks and shivering shocks shall break the locks
> >Of prison gates ;
> And Phibbus' car shall shine from far, and make and mar
> >The foolish fates.

Or another may print them as full undivided verses. The manner of printing does not destroy the units; the same stanza-unit may appear under many guises, giving pleasure to the eye as well as to the ear. So, for all the intricate rime-music of the two following, the lilt of the ordinary stanza comes clearly to the ear:

> What needs complaints,
> >When she a place
> >Hath with the race
> >>Of saints?
> In endless mirth,
> >She thinks not on
> >What's said or done
> >>In earth.
> >>>(Herrick, *Comfort to a youth....*)

> Love, I recant,
> And pardon crave
> That lately I offended,
> >But 'twas,
> >>Alas,
> To make a brave,
> But no disdain intended.
> >>(Herrick, *His recantation*, st. 1.)

Both are full Ballad verses:

> What needs complaints, when she a place
> >Hath with the race of saints?
> In endless mirth, she thinks not on
> >What's said or done in earth.

> Love, I recant, and pardon crave
> >That lately I offended,
> But 'twas, alas, to make a brave,
> >But no disdain intended.

In the extreme form of this division of the verse, each
stress-unit becomes a line:

> Thus I
> Pass by
> And die,
> As one
> Unknown
> And gone;
> I'm made
> A shade
> And laid
> I' th' grave,
> There have
> My cave.
> Where tell
> I dwell,
> Farewell.
>
> (Herrick, *Upon his departure hence*.)

This is composed of two Alexandrines and a half:

> Thus I pass by and die, as one unknown and gone;
> I'm made a shade and laid i' th' grave, there have my cave.
> Where tell I dwell, Farewell.

Here, again, the thoughts and the verses are coterminous.

The influence of the refrain in the evolution of the
stanza-unit must have been considerable; but consideration of this must be deferred.

CHAPTER VI

POETRY AND MUSIC

WHILST it has been stated that the musical scansion suggested by Lanier is unsatisfactory because the symbols of music are too definite to be applied to the syllables making up stress-units, there is no doubt that music and poetry were once much more closely allied than they now are.

The fact that many of the old dance-tunes have the same names as ballads shews that ballads were sung to accompany dances. It is probable that there were, as there still are amongst the Maori of New Zealand, two kinds of singing; one rhythmical only, as heard in their laments, love-songs, and lullabies, and one perfectly metrical. The former may be accompanied with swaying, and motion of the arms, quivering of the hands; the latter is accompanied with dance.

In *English Minstrelsie* Gould says that the introduction of the fiddle banished the ballad as a song-accompaniment to the dance, but that for a time the dancers sang whilst moving to the sounds of the instrument. A series of these Folk-dance-songs opens a volume of the Danish poet Ingemann.

Apparently dancing effected the introduction of "time" into the old tunes, or perhaps only hastened its development, and no doubt the old rhythmical tunes would undergo considerable transformation when being rendered with the sense of time regulating their utterance. That the ballads themselves were altered considerably when changing from the rhythmical to

the metrical form is shewn well in the two forms of
The Battle of Chevy Chase contained in the collection
of the Percy ballads, and of these two forms no doubt
the earlier is much more nearly metrical than still
earlier unrecorded forms. Musical instruments have now
almost altogether supplanted the voice in accompanying
dance, but an approach, if a distant one, is occasionally
made even at the present day ; when the dancers, caught
by some favourite melody happily introduced by the
orchestra or pianist, break into subdued song as they
dance, a pleasure only too rarely enjoyed.

In *English Minstrelsie* is given a list of ninety-five
dance-tunes published by Playford in 1651. Their names
shew them to have been ballads, and the words of
thirty of these ballads are known. To some of the
others later words have been set, supplanting the
original ones.

The ruggedness of many a stanza is smoothed out
when it is learned that it is a song, and the tune is
known; without its music what but a lame conclusion
could be made of the following?—

> Charon, make haste, and ferry me over
>   to the Elysian shady grove,
> Where I my passion in sighs will discover,
>   which I have suffered long for love;
> I am weary of my life, and cannot be eased, no,
>   nowhere;
> Then put a period to my grief, and carry me where I may
>   know no care.
>
> (P[ocock], *The despairing Lover's address to Charon*, st. 1.)

The tune to which this song was sung was *Charon,
make haste*; and to the same tune was sung the
following:

> Chloe, your unrelenting scorn
>   has been too lasting, and severe;
> No truth but mine could e'er have borne
>   the tortures of so long despair.
> Those unkind words your rage replied
>   to what my hand and heart had given,
> Shewed not your virtue, but your pride:
>   Love may expostulate with Heaven.
>
> *(The languishing Swain*, st. 1.)

These two differing rhythms are reconciled by the melody. There are fifteen ballads known to have been sung to the tune of *The languishing Swain*, one of these being, *I loved you dearly, I loved you well*. There are five other ballads to the tune of *I loved you dearly...*, one being, *All happy times, when free from love*, and there are five others to the tune, *All happy times....* There are six to the tune *Charon, make haste*, and four to the tune of *The false-hearted young man,* an alternative title of *The languishing Swain;*—in all, thirty-two known ballads to the same tune. The differences in rhythm are explicable when it is remembered that these ballads were often written by illiterate people; and one of the most prolific of these writers, a weaver, could ballet only " when fortified with ale." Liberty might also be taken with the music, as noted by Gould, yet the norm of the tune survived through all vicissitudes. Again, on one metrical scheme, the rhythm of the verses floating upon it may vary so much that prosodists find a difficulty in agreeing as to what that scheme is; —were the tune not known, how much more would they disagree as to the scheme to which such diverse stanzas as the above could be accommodated?

It is, perhaps, unjust to ascribe altogether to illiteracy the varying rhythms that go to particular tunes, for the same liberty is taken by the literate also. The best of writers, when music other than the silently-flowing music of metre is in their minds, will occasionally use words that, without the music, do not conform to natural verse-units:

> Come to me in the silence of the night;
>   Come in the speaking silence of a dream;
> Come with soft rounded cheeks and eyes as bright
>   As sunlight on a stream;
>   Come back in tears,
> O memory, hope, love of vanished years.
> (C. Rossetti, Echo, st. 1.)

It is almost certain, from the construction of this lovely poem, that it was written for music,—and for music already known to the poet;—it does not sing its own music as, say, Herrick's stanzas do; and without knowledge of the special melody, it would be impossible to know that, with the melody, it sings into a perfectly balanced lyric stanza:

> Còme to mè in the sìlence of the nìght;
>   Còme in the spèaking silence òf a drèam;
> Còme with soft ròunded cheeks ànd eyes as brìght
>   Às sunlight òn a strèam.....
> Còme back in tèars...còme back in tèars,
>   Ò memory, hòpe, love of vànished yèars.

These stresses correspond with the main accents as they fall in the music, the short line is repeated as above, and the whole song is very beautiful. Other stresses

and accents than these may be made in reading;
—perhaps no two readers will make the same stresses,
—nor need they.

In this analysis it is merely wished to shew how the
irregular verses are sung as a lyric stanza;—there is
nothing urged against it or many similar beautiful
creations; a writer, with a certain tune in mind, may
produce a perfect stanza that, to one ignorant of the
tune, may appear unmetrical, or may appear to be in
quite another metre.

In the same way, a stanza in the least different from
the norm may appear irregular, unmetrical, to one in
whom the silent temporal music of poetry beats faintly,
and who therefore needs the aid of regularity to perceive the metre. This is one reason why regular Heroics
such as Pope's have wider appeal than the varied Blanks
of Milton; why Lyrics regularly two or three-syllabled, or with two and three-syllabled units regularly
blended, are more popular than those varied by pauses
and irregular rhythms such as many of Christina
Rossetti's.

It must be observed that the song *Echo* has been
scanned by Professor Saintsbury in quite a different
way. His scansion makes it assume verses of five units,
not lyric lines of four:

> Come to / me in / the si/lence of / the night;
> Come in / the speak/ing si/lence of / a dream;

To the present writer this does not feel comfortable.

Again, without its tune, now known through the
British world and overflowing its borders, could the
following possibly be read as a regular stanza?

There's a long, long trail a-winding
　　Into the land of my dreams,
Where the nightingales are singing
　　And a white moon beams:
There's a long, long night of waiting
　　Until my dreams all come true,
Till the day when I'll be going
　　Down that long, long trail with you.

Even in the writing down of the stanza the intensity
of its feeling surged up again;—but were the song
preserved without its tune, might not some prosodist
in the centuries to come use it as argument against
the correct ear of the present time?

Since music has such a powerful influence in transforming the rhythm of words, parallels of construction
might be expected when the rhythm of the two is in
complete accord. Ouseley, in writing on Melody,
mentions tonality as the first fundamental principle,
symmetry as the second; it is in symmetry that music
and poetry agree. Every regular melody may be divided
into Periods, Phrases, and Strains. These Ouseley calls
the prosody of music. He illustrates these terms by
quoting the beginning of the Huntsman's Chorus in
Weber's *Der Freyschuetz*:

This, taken altogether, is a Period—a complete sentence ending with a full stop. It is divided into two Phrases of equal length, and each Phrase is divided into two equal Strains. The Strains are marked by brackets placed over the notes; the Phrases by longer brackets placed under them. "Here," observes Ouseley, "we obviously have perfect symmetry and regularity throughout the whole Period."

In this melody, every bar contains two crotchets, or their temporal equivalent, and there are eight bars. In lyric metre, every full verse contains eight units, and every stress unit contains two syllables or their temporal equivalent. Every verse, too, is usually a complete sentence, divided into two main clauses, the clauses again divided, in many instances, into sub-clauses.

This simple basis is the basis upon which all lyric music and poetry are built. In dance music especially the basis is most apparent; and in the Quadrille, long a popular dance, the full melody for every figure of the dance consists of thirty-two bars, four equal parts of eight bars each. The dance is performed by separate sets each of eight people, and these in every figure weave, as it were, the equivalent of a stanza of eight lines, each line with four units,—a Romance-eight in fact. All the set dances are in melodies of thirty-two bars, like the quadrille, and practically all dances are built on eight-bar themes, as all lyric poems are on eight-unit verses.

Supposing the rhythm of the above melody were reduced to a monotone; that is, supposing the notes were tapped, instead of being sung;—it will be found that the tune will still be recognized. This means that this melody, and most melodies, have a rhythmic as well as a melodic individuality by which they may be recognized. This has been made the source of a regular game. One person taps a tune, the other guesses it, and taps in his turn. Even individual stanzas, individual verses of poetry, possess this characteristic in a lesser degree, and the words of a verse may often be recalled by tapping its rhythm over and over. It is also a fact that poetry, more especially dramatic blank verse, has a melodic as well as a rhythmic individuality.

It must be repeated, however, that the difference between the syllabic rhythm of poetry and the note rhythm of music is great, and it is this: in music the individual notes have fixed values from which, as a rule, they do not vary in any one piece, all bars being normally equal; in poetry, the value of the syllables, which represent the notes, is quite unfixed, their individual temporal value varying according to vowel and consonant composition in a minor degree, and according to the number contained in a unit in a major degree. In music it is usual that a crotchet is a crotchet, a quaver a quaver; occasionally three crotchets may be taken in the time of two, four in the time of three, and so on, but this is so unusual that a special indication of the variation is always given. In poetry the syllables vary infinitely; a syllable may now represent a quaver, now a dotted quaver, a crotchet, a dotted crotchet,—the variation is so perpetual that no indication of it is given,—it is the normal condition. The stress-units are fairly equal in temporal value, but not with the regularity of bars of music.

His insistence on the musical regularity of poetry makes much of Sidney Lanier's prosodic theory

untenable. It is dangerous to represent the rhythm of
poetry by musical notation, or indeed by any system
of symbols. He has chosen his examples and given his
illustrations usually with such care, that often, in reading
his fascinating volume, one is almost persuaded; but
here and there are examples that arouse entire dissent.
His setting of *The Raven* is one; his setting of *The
Psalm of Life* is another. Of this he gives the time-values
of the syllables as follows:

Tell   me not   in mourn-ful num-bers Life   is but   an

emp - ty dream.

Were the syllables sung to a melody, they might be
arranged to these definite values; but in ordinary speech
they are not;—in the reading of poetry they are not.
It may be conceded that some would read them in
this way; but a great many would not. Compare the
above with the well-known songs *Jock o' Hazeldean* and
Ye Banks and Braes. Is either of these spoken or recited
as sung? No; music has its definite time-values, and
in the art-song these values are arranged more in
accord with the natural speech-values. The ordinary
distribution of the values is far more intricate than the
simple alternation of crotchet and quaver, or crotchet
and crotchet. Song imposes what values it will on the
words; it compels the words to conform to itself; speech
or reading compels the time to conform to the words.
Most readers will say "Tell me" to the time ♪ ♩ rather
than to ♩ ♪; "numbers" to the time ♪ ♩ rather than
to ♩ ♪—and would even one reader give "but" the

value of the words "Tell" or "mourn" or "dream"?
Further, different readers will give different values to
the words. Dr Thomson in his recent book *The Rhythm
of Speech*, suggests that arbitrary signs may be given
for the various values employed. Experience seems to
prove otherwise; for whilst Lanier suggests ♩ ♪ for
"numbers," and the writer feels ♪ ♩ more natural,
another may feel ♪. ♪. more natural, and there may be
an infinity of intermediate variations in the three values,
—and this was meant when it was said that the iamb
might vary from ⏑ ⏑ to ‿ ‿, and the trochee from ‿ ⏑
to ‿ ‿. This infinite variation within the unit is its
characteristic quality;—the stress-units are themselves
temporally comparatively equal, but the constituents
of the units may be assembled in kaleidophonic variety,
—and it is this which gives the charm of hover and
hurry that renders individual so many lines and verses
of poetry.

It is preferable to avoid signs with definite values,
for the reason that the definite values of the individual
syllables do not exist as does the temporal value of
the stress-unit;—if therefore the verse is printed:

Tèll me nòt in mòurnful nùmbers Lìfe is but an èmpty drèam

the reader, providing he observe the temporal equality
of the units, is at liberty to distribute the values of the
syllables at will,—and it is this varying distribution
that results in the varying readings of individuals, each
one interpreting the rhythm as best pleases his ear.

As has been said, it is this individuality of the time-
values, this personality of rhythm, to which Saintsbury

gives the name "fingering." It is this fingering that gives its music to poetry; it awakens the perceptions to the enormously wide possibilities of rhythm;—it reunites the two that have for a time been separated, for it is the rhythm of the poem itself that influences the better musician when he sets his music to the words, not the words to his music. It must be confessed, too, that it is this individuality that has caused much discussion among prosodists;—it is the point on which they appear to differ most. The reason is, each would suppose his own distribution of the individual time-values to be the correct one. Much difference of opinion will disappear if it is recognized that it is the division of the lyric verse into eight stress-units comparatively equal in temporal value that is fundamental; the distribution of the syllabic time-values within the stress-unit is optional.

CHAPTER VII

CLASSIFICATION

IT is now desirable to shew how the verse-unit and the stanza-unit may be taken as guides for the classification of British lyric poetry; and, were it desired, of lyric poetry other than British also.

The type-verse is a verse of eight stress-units or their temporal equivalents. The usual forms of the verse-unit assumed by the type are four:

1. Romance: A verse of eight stress-units; two, three, or four-syllabled.
2. Ballad: A verse of seven stress-units; two, three, or four-syllabled.
3. Nibelungen: A verse of six stress-units; two, three, or four-syllabled.
4. Alexandrine: A verse of six stress-units; two, three, or four-syllabled.

In Ballad, Nibelungen, and Alexandrine, the eighth unit is silent, this being the place of taking the breath. In Nibelungen, one half of the fourth unit, and in Alexandrine, the whole of the fourth unit, is unsyllabled, and occupied by a sonant hover or pause. The four forms, in two-syllabled rhythm, are represented as follows, dots taking the place of syllables:

1. Romance: 𝅘𝅥𝅘𝅥𝅘𝅥𝅘𝅥 𝅘𝅥𝅘𝅥𝅘𝅥𝅘𝅥
2. Ballad: 𝅘𝅥𝅘𝅥𝅘𝅥𝅘𝅥 𝅘𝅥𝅘𝅥𝅘𝅥 ।
3. Nibelungen: 𝅘𝅥𝅘𝅥𝅘𝅥·। 𝅘𝅥𝅘𝅥𝅘𝅥 ।
4. Alexandrine: 𝅘𝅥𝅘𝅥𝅘𝅥 । 𝅘𝅥𝅘𝅥𝅘𝅥 ।

In Romance, a tendency to take a breath at the mid-verse has created a slight pause that still persists in all four; but in the last three the breath is taken easily in the eighth unit, whilst in Romance it is a short breath after the eighth.

In all the four units certain regular as well as irregular variations occur. The irregular variations consist of slightly increasing or decreasing the number of syllables in the stress-units, and the arbitrary mingling of such units. Two stanzas from Shelley's *Sensitive Plant* are quoted as illustration:

A sènsitive plànt in a gàrden grèw,
And the yòung wìnds fèd it with sìlver dèw,
And it òpened its fàn-lìke lèaves to the lìght,
And clòsed them benèath the kìsses of nìght.

And the Sprìng aròse on the gàrden fàir,
Like the Spìrit of Lòve felt èverywhère;
And each flòwer and hèrb on Èarth's dàrk brèast
Ròse from the drèams of its wìntry rèst.

(*Sensitive Plant*, Part 1, st. 1 and 2.)

The blending is best heard by the ear when the words are repeated; it is best seen by the eye when the syllables are represented by dots, the best realized when the number of syllables in the consecutive units is given as below:

2 3 3 2 syllables.

3 2 3 2 „

3 3 2 3 „

2 3 2 3 „

··᠄ ᠄··᠄ ᠄   3 2 3 2 syllables.
··᠄··᠄ ᠄ ᠄   3 3 2 2   „
··᠄ ᠄ ᠄ ᠄   3 2 2 2   „
᠄··᠄··᠄ ᠄   1 3 3 2   „

In all eight lines, two only have the two-syllabled and three-syllabled units in the same order,—the second in the first stanza and the first in the second. As great a diversity as in these two stanzas will be found throughout the poem; there is no regularity in the syllabic irregularity; the order of the differing units follows no rule; it is altogether dependent upon the individual inclination of the writer; it is, in fact, the source of distinctive rhythms, infinite in their variety. There are, however, other irregularities that are regular in their occurrence: these are found at the verse openings, but chiefly at the two main pauses—the mid-pause and verse-end. They occur with the most perceptible and definite frequency in the breath-pause at the verse-end, and with less definiteness or less frequency at the mid-verse, or *line*-end, their definiteness being greatly increased by the occurrence of rime. Variation at these points is also dependent upon the inclination of the writer, in so far that he is at liberty to employ them or not as he pleases; but should his verse-end shew a certain variation, anticipation expects the variation in the following verse also, and is more satisfied when the repetition takes place. For instance, when Byron wrote:

> The serpent of the field, by art
>   And spells is won from harming;
> But that which coils around the heart,
>   Oh! who hath power of charming?
> It will not list to wisdom's lore,
>   Nor music's voice can lure it;
> But there it stings for evermore
>   The soul that must endure it.
>   (Lord Byron, *All is Vanity, saith the Preacher*, st. 3.)

he introduced a variation by adding a syllable to the verse-end:

> The serpent of the field, by art
>   And spells is won from harm*ing*;
> But that which coils around the heart,
>   Oh! who hath power of charm*ing*?

The verses are complete without the italicized syllable; but having added it to the first verse, it was called for in the second, and in a less degree, in the third and fourth; it became, in fact, a regular irregularity or variation. A similar variation at the *line*-end is seen in Landor's stanza:

> Graceful Acacia! slender, brittle,
>   I think I know the like of thee;
> But thou art tall and she is little—
>   What God shall call her his own tree?
> Some God must be the last to change her;
>   From him alone she will not flee;
> O may he fix to earth the ranger,
>   And may he lend her shade to me.
>   (W. S. Landor, No. vi. of *The Last Fruit off an Old Tree*.)

He has added a syllable to the first line-end as Byron added one to the first verse-end; and the very fact that he has added it to the corresponding line-ends shews that he was conscious of an expectancy that should not be disappointed. The riming increases the expectancy.

The following example clearly shews that the poet is fully conscious of the expectation aroused by this variation:

> A key no thief can steal, no time can rust;
>   A faery door, adventurous and golden;
> A palace, perfect to our eyes—ah! must
>   Our eyes be holden?
>
> Has the past died before this present sin?
>   Has this most cruel age already stonèd
> To martyrdom that magic Day, within
>   Those halls, enthronèd?
>
>   (Stella Benson, *Christmas*, 1917, st. 1, 2.)

There was no *necessity* for "stonèd" and "enthronèd," but the first stanza aroused an expectation, however slight, and this expectation is met, even though an unusual rime results.

As observed, these irregularities are made definite by the rime: the irregularities at the *opening* of the line are different. If the rhythm be regularly two-syllabled, the opening unit will usually contain two syllables; but if irregular like Shelley's poem above, the opening unit may vary from one to three syllables. If the rhythm be regularly three-syllabled, the opening unit will usually contain two or three syllables. In two-syllabled and three-syllabled rhythm, if the opening unit contain only one syllable, the stressed one, the rhythm is considered as changed from the ordinary (iambic or anapaestic) to the trochaic or dactylic. Usually, but by no means necessarily, if a poem opens with a trochee it is trochaic throughout.

These three comparatively regular variations are taken as the index of "varieties" in stanza forms. The forms are first divided into two great groups, iambic-anapaestic, and trochaic-dactylic, according as the verse begins with unstressed or stressed syllables. The verse-end, as the most important from its greater definiteness, distinguishes the varieties in these two groups,—the line-end, and varied opening in iambic-anapaestic rhythm, making sub-varieties. The two-syllabled being taken as the natural type of unit, the natural Romance verse will be a two-syllabled verse of eight stress-units:

$$\acute{}| \ \acute{}| \ \acute{}| \ \acute{}| \quad \acute{}| \ \acute{}| \ \acute{}| \ \acute{}|$$

This, expanding in all its units, becomes the three-syllabled type:

$$\cdot\acute{}| \ \cdot\acute{}| \ \cdot\acute{}| \ \cdot\acute{}| \quad \cdot\acute{}| \ \cdot\acute{}| \ \cdot\acute{}| \ \cdot\acute{}|$$

Here each dot represents a syllable, the bars below being wave-crests, or stress-points of the metre, the accent-marks being the place of the accented syllables. In the metre, it will be remembered, the units are of comparatively equal temporal value, so that the metre is the even beating of the stresses. The rhythm is brought about by the omission or addition of a syllable here and there, or the insertion of heavier syllables, accented or otherwise, or the creation of hovers in varying positions, the irregular rhythm floating perfectly upon the regular underlying metre. It is through different rhythms that the two-syllabled Romance verse may expand to the three-syllabled and four-syllabled, as shewn below, where the intermediate forms —two and three-syllabled units mingled—are omitted:

a. [notation] (2, 2, 2, 2, 2, 2, 2, 2.)

b. [notation] (2, 3, 3, 3, 2, 3, 3, 3.)

c. [notation] (2, 3, 3, 3, 3, 3, 3, 3.)

d. [notation] (2, 4, 4, 4, 2, 4, 4, 4.)

e. [notation] (2, 4, 4, 4, 3, 4, 4, 4.)

f. [notation] (2, 4, 4, 4, 4, 4, 4, 4.)

g. [notation] (3, 3, 3, 3, 2, 3, 3, 3.)

h. [notation] (3, 3, 3, 3, 3, 3, 3, 3.)

i. [notation] (3, 4, 4, 4, 2, 4, 4, 4.)

j. [notation] (3, 4, 4, 4, 3, 4, 4, 4.)

k. [notation] (3, 4, 4, 4, 4, 4, 4, 4.)

l. [notation] (4, 4, 4, 4, 2, 4, 4, 4.)

m. [notation] (4, 4, 4, 4, 3, 4, 4, 4.)

n. [notation] (4, 4, 4, 4, 4, 4, 4, 4.)

These variations are slight in appearance, but they are regular, especially in the two-syllabled and three-syllabled forms, where they constitute the basic verse-forms of entire stanzas. Examples of the more regular forms follow:

    (*a*) O they rade on, and farther on, the steed gaed swifter
        than the wind;
       Until they reached a desart wide, and living land was
        left behind...
                          (*Thomas the Rhymer*, st. 9.)

    (*b*) My heart's in the Highlands, my heart is not here,
        my heart's in the Highlands a-chasing the deer,
      A-chasing the wild deer and following the roe—
        my heart's in the Highlands wherever I go!
                (R. Burns, *My heart's in the Highlands*.)

(*c*) Twelve years have elapsed since I last took a view
          of my favourite field, and the bank where they grew;
       And now in the grass behold they are laid,
          and the tree is my seat that once lent a shade.

                              (W. Cowper, *The Poplars*, st. 2.)

This stanza is irregular in so far that it contains two
two-syllabled units,—the third and the seventh in the
second verse; but such internal irregularity is common;
it is the "fingering" of the rhythm, and does not affect
the type.

(*d*) And how the happy Earth, growing young again in mirth,
          has prank't herself in jewels to do honour to the day.
       Of gold and purple bright, of azure and of white;
          her diadem and bracelets, the meadow flowers of May.

                    (C. Mackay, *'Tis merry in the Mead*, part stanza 2.)

(*e*) Like the bright light that shone in Kildare's holy fane,
          and burned through long ages of darkness and storm,
       Is the heart that sorrows have frowned on in vain,
          whose spirit outlives them, unfading and warm.

                              (T. Moore, *Erin, O Erin*, st. 1.)

(*f*) The Assyrian came down like a wolf on the fold,
          and his cohorts were gleaming in purple and gold,
       And the sheen of their spears was like stars on the sea,
          when the blue wave rolls nightly on deep Galilee.

                    (Lord Byron, *The Destruction of Sennacherib*, st. 1.)

These verses may vary again, in two ways, at the
mid-verse; the second half may open with the stressed
syllable; or the first half may end with an extra
unaccented syllable, making a feminine ending:

             𝅘𝅥𝅘𝅥𝅘𝅥𝅘𝅥 𝅘𝅥𝅘𝅥𝅘𝅥𝅘𝅥   (2, 2, 2, 2, 1, 2, 2, 2.)

             𝅘𝅥𝅘𝅥𝅘𝅥𝅘𝅥· 𝅘𝅥𝅘𝅥𝅘𝅥𝅘𝅥   (2, 2, 2, 2⁺, 2, 2, 2, 2.)

and so through the various openings shewn above. The
former variation is of infrequent occurrence; it appears

more in isolated verses; rarely, if ever, in complete stanzas. There appears to be a repugnance for an abrupt (or trochaic) second half to follow a half-verse with ordinary (or iambic) opening. Were the word "each" in the following example omitted, the verse would represent the type:

> The drawbridge falls—they hurry out—
> Clatters (each) plank and swinging chain.
> (Sir W. Scott, Cadyow Castle, st. 11.)

It is represented in three-syllabled rhythm by:

> The year's at the spring and day's at the morn;
> morning's at seven; the hillside's dewpearled;
> The lark's on the wing; the snail's on the thorn:
> God's in his heaven—all's right with the world.
> (R. Browning, from Pippa Passes.)

> I have read her romances of dame and knight;
> she was my princess, my pride, my pet.
> (A. L. Gordon, The Romance of Britomart.)

Gordon's poem contains several examples of the rhythm, but all admit two-syllabled units. The variation shewing a feminine ending to the first half of the verse is much more frequently met with: examples in two-syllabled, three-syllabled, and four-syllabled rhythm follow:

> When lovely woman stoops to folly,
> and finds too late that men betray,
> What charm can soothe her melancholy,
> what art can wash her guilt away?
> (O. Goldsmith, Stanzas on Woman.)

> How long didst thou think that his silence was slumber?
> When the wind waved his garment, how oft didst thou start?
> How many days long and long weeks didst thou number,
> ere he faded before thee, the friend of thy heart?
> (Sir W. Scott, Helvellyn, part st. 3.)

Of the mail-cover'd barons, who proudly to battle
    led their vassals from Europe to Palestine's plain,
The escutcheon and shield, which with every blast rattle,
    are the only sad vestiges now that remain.
          (Lord Byron, *On leaving Newstead Abbey*, st. 2.)

There's a cry from out the loneliness—Oh listen, Honey,
    listen!
Do you hear it, do you fear it, you're a-holding of me so?
You're a-sobbing in your sleep, dear, and your lashes how
    they glisten—
Do you hear the Little Voices all a-begging me to go?
          (R. W. Service, *The Little Voices.*)

I bless them but I'm sad for them—I wish I could be glad for
    them,
    for who alas! can tell me the fate that shall befall?
The flow'rets of the morning, the greenwood path adorning,
    may be scatter'd ere the noontide by the wild wind's
    sudden call.
    (C. Mackay, *Flowers and Children*, Fifth line from opening.)

There are occasional examples of double-feminine endings; these would form a small class, similar to the class with ordinary feminine endings, and they have been classed with the simple feminine endings.

In the foregoing examples verses have been selected whose structure is as regular as possible;—regular, that is, in so far that a two-syllabled verse is composed of two-syllabled units; a three-syllabled verse of three-syllabled, and so on. In all poetry there is a *tendency* towards regularity of this kind, so that a type may be established in the mind,—though once the type is established, the units may vary syllabically. The formal school, usually connected with the names of Pope and

Dryden, almost insisted upon the necessity for this regularity; but the fact that poets gifted with keener vision and more facile utterance than either Pope or Dryden, shewed repeatedly that the best poetry could be conveyed in irregular verse, is conclusive proof that whilst the *tendency* towards syllabic regularity exists, the *necessity* for it does not. There should be temporal equality, and it is the very existence of this that seems to call for syllabic numerical equality also, lest one unit should seem disproportioned: this is especially true when the temporal music beats faintly. A great many readers receive more pleasure from a syllabically regular than from a syllabically irregular verse, for with the temporal music beating faintly the irregularity becomes obtrusive.

Coleridge's *Christabel* is largely irregular; still more typically so is Shelley's *Sensitive Plant*. When Leigh Hunt, in 1835, first published his *Captain Sword and Captain Pen*, he found it necessary to remark in the advertisement,—"The measure is regular with an irregular aspect, four accents in a verse, like that of Christabel, or some of the poems of Sir Walter Scott:

> Càptain Swòrd got ùp one dày—
> And the flàg full of hònour as thòugh it could fèel—

He [the author] mentions this, not, of course, for readers in general, but for the sake of those daily acceders to the list of the reading public, whose knowledge of books is not yet equal to their love of them." Though this development was regarded by many as new, it was not new, though perhaps unusual in the better kind of poetry; it had always been present in the "tumbling" rhythms. The original constitution of the unit was irregular; and, in addition, the underlying metre had not assumed its regular temporal proportions. Purely two-syllabled or purely three-syllabled verses were then not only desirable, but almost necessary, in order that the temporal periods might be perceived. Once they were perceived, however, the syllables might again vary; one here, two there, or three; or syllables might be altogether absent; but the metre flowed on, and flows on, unbroken and regular. The second great group differs from the first in the last unit only. This unit may have a feminine ending. The variations and sub-variations of both groups are identical, and it will not therefore be necessary to quote more than a few examples:

> And is she dead?—and did they dare
>   obey my frenzy's jealous raving?
> My wrath but doom'd my own despair:
>   the sword that smote her's o'er me waving.
>   (Lord Byron, *Herod's Lament for Mariamne*, st. 2.)
>
> Oh may it prove for Scotland's good!
>   bonnie laddie, Highland laddie,
> But why so drench our glens with blood?
>   bonnie laddie, Highland laddie.
>   (James Hogg, *Highland Laddie*, last stanza.)
>
> Her voice did quiver as we parted,
>   yet knew I not that heart was broken
> From whence it came, and I departed
>   heeding not the words then spoken.
>   (P. B. Shelley, *On Fanny Godwin*.)

A sub-group of the second differs from the first and second in the last unit only, which has a *double* feminine ending. It is seldom met with except in humorous poetry, and even then the perfect form occurs only in occasional verses:

> And e'en as Macbeth, when devising the death
>   of his king heard "the very stones prate of his
>   whereabouts;"
> So this shocking bad wife heard a voice all her
>   life crying "Murder!" resound from the
>   cushion—or thereabouts.
>
> > (R. H. Barham, *A Lay of St Gengulmus*, st. 73.)
>
> Her little red eyes were deep-set in their
>   socket-holes, her gown-tail was turn'd up,
>   and tuck'd through the pocket-holes.
>
> > (R. H. Barham, *Look at the Clock*, sec. 1.)
>
> And a tenderer leveret Robin had never ate;
>   so, in after times, oft he was wont to asseverate.
>
> > (R. H. Barham, *The Witches' Frolic*.)

The foregoing groups comprise Division 1 of Romance metre. Division 2 has similar groups, with their variations exactly as in Division 1. The two Divisions are distinguished by the *first* unit of the verse. All iambic-anapaestic two, three, and four-syllabled openings belong to Division 1; all trochaic-dactylic openings to Division 2. A few examples from Division 2 will suffice:

> Aske me why I send you here this sweet Infanta
>   of the yeare?
> Aske me why I send to you this Primrose
>   thus bepearl'd with dew?
>
> > (R. Herrick, *The Primrose*, st. 1.)
>
> He that loves a rosy cheek, or a coral lip admires,
> Or from star-like eyes doth seek fuel to maintain its fires:
>
> > (T. Carew, *He that loves....*)

God be with thee, gladsome Ocean;
   how gladly greet I thee once more!
Ships and waves and ceaseless motion,
   and men rejoicing on thy shore.
        (S. T. Coleridge, *On revisiting the Sea-shore*, st. 1.)

Annan Water's wading deep,
   and my love Annie's wondrous bonny:
I will keep my tryst to-night,
   and win the heart of lovely Annie.
        (Annan Water, st. 1.)

Ballad, Nibelungen, and Alexandrine metres vary
in the same way, though not to the same extent. It
may be noted that should a Romance verse *drop* its
last syllable (stressed), it is no longer Romance, but
feminine Ballad; should it drop the last syllable
(stressed) of the first half-verse, it becomes that peculiar
and uncommon verse found as the "swell" in Nibelungen stanzas. Should a Ballad verse drop the last
syllable (stressed) of the first half-verse, it becomes
Nibelungen; and should a Nibelungen verse drop the
last syllable (unstressed) of the first half-verse, it becomes Alexandrine;—as too does a Ballad verse which
drops the last unit of the first half-verse. The unpaused
Alexandrine is formed, not by the dropping of the last
unit of a Ballad verse, but by the crushing out of the
central hover of the ordinary Alexandrine.

The whole of the variations of the Romance verse,
and there are over a hundred, may be expressed in the
single symbolized verse following:

$$(.)(.)(.)\wr(.)(.)(.)\wr(.)(.)(.)\wr(.)(.)(.)\wr(.)(.)$$
$$(.)(.)(.)\wr(.)(.)(.)\wr(.)(.)(.)\wr(.)(.)(.)\wr(.)(.)$$

Here the points within brackets represent syllables
that may or may not be present, the two syllables

following the last stress of each line or half-verse representing feminine and double feminine endings. On first glance and first thought this may appear no better than chaos; but a minute's patience will reveal the perfect orderliness of the underlying scheme.

Drop a regular number of syllables, say two, from each unit, always dropping those more remote from the following stress, and the ordinary Romance verse will appear:

$$(\cdot)\ \text{♩♩♩♩} \quad (\cdot)\ \text{♩♩♩♩}$$

In the same way drop one syllable instead of two, and the three-syllabled Romance will appear:

$$(\cdot)\text{♩·♩·♩·♩} \quad (\cdot)\text{♩·♩·♩·♩}$$

In both these the feminine endings have also been dropped. Drop these feminine endings only, and the four-syllabled Romance will appear:

$$(\cdot)(\cdot)\text{♩··♩··♩··♩} \quad (\cdot)(\cdot)\text{♩··♩··♩··♩}$$

Should an irregular number of syllables be dropped,— that is, two from one unit, one from another, now here, now there, at haphazard, the intermediate forms, the "tumbling verse," will appear:

$$(\cdot)\ \text{♩·♩♩♩ ♩♩·♩♩}$$

This is the form intermediate between the two-syllabled and the three-syllabled;—the form of Shelley's *Sensitive Plant*.

With four-syllabled units:

$$\text{♩·♩··♩♩ ··♩♩·♩··♩}$$

This is the form intermediate between the two-syllabled and four-syllabled, three-syllabled units also appearing; —the form of C. Rossetti's *Amor Mundi*, of Meredith's *Love in a Valley*,—delightful creations.

The more than a hundred forms represented in the

verse first set out divide quite naturally into a series of
distinct classes, each with its distinct subdivisions.
They first divide into two great classes. As these are
distinguished by their first unit only, the first two units
only need be shewn, the others being exactly similar
to those of the verse first set out:

Units

1. (.)(.)⸜(.)(.)⸜

2.   ⸜(.)(.)⸜

In the first are included all verses whose opening unit
is iambic-anapaestic, in the second all verses whose
opening unit is trochaic-dactylic.

Each of these again gives rise to a sub-class distinguished by the *last* unit. Shewing the first, second,
and last units only, these are:

Units

1A. (.)(.)⸜(.)(.)⸜   (.)(.)⸜

2A.   ⸜(.)(.)⸜   (.)(.)⸜

These differ from the parent forms only in the dropping
of the final feminine.

This gives four classes, and each of these four again
gives rise to three forms, distinguished at the *mid*-verse:

Units

a. (.)(.)⸜(.)(.)   ⸜(.)(.)⸜

b. (.)(.)⸜   (.)(.)⸜(.)(.)⸜

c. (.)(.)⸜   ⸜(.)(.)⸜

This variation may appear in each of the four forms
above, Classes 1 and 2 and Sub-classes 1A and 2A,
the result being the production of twelve distinct forms.

The twelve forms, again, may all vary in the manner
shewn at page 189;—that is, the iambic-anapaestic forms

may have as many as fourteen minor variations when the verse and half-verse end with an accented syllable; the addition of feminine and double feminine endings trebles the number. The variations of the trochaic-dactylic forms are not so great in number, as the first unit cannot vary.

The whole of these again may vary by being in "tumbling verse" instead of being regularly two, three, or four-syllabled.

The enormous amount of varying rhythm this allows will be evident; but it must be observed that the bulk of British poetry employs a comparatively small number of the variations; and as the subdivisions become more minute, they are more mingled. It is quite possible, however, to write perfectly regular and readable stanzas in every one of them. A complete Table of the variations is not given here; it may easily be compiled by anyone curious enough to see the regular flowing of variation from variation.

Nor is the subdivision as complicated as it appears to be. The whole of the variations of A2 are the same as those of A1 except in the first unit;—one starts with unaccented syllables, the other with accented syllables. So too of the other forms; they run in pairs; but slight as the differences are, they are observed by writers, more or less strictly according to the keenness of their perception of rhythm.

The following Tables shew how the many stanza-forms likewise flow from one simple basic form; and when the possible number of stanza forms is seen, and it is realized that all of them may be written in any of the foregoing rhythms, it will also be realized that the possible variations in the rhythm of our poetry are practically infinite, and that so far only the fringe of the number, as it were, has been touched.

Whilst a great many stanzas appear to be irregular in form, it will be seen from the following Tables that a great part of the seeming irregularity is regular variation. This has already been partly shewn in Chapter V. This Table is a scheme of possible variations, though it must be observed that by no means all of these variations occur. The Table is intended merely as a guide shewing the kinship of stanza-variations, and their derivation from a common source:

Stanza forms.

Lines	1	2	3	4	
A1	4	4	4	4	units
2	4	4	4	3	,,
3	4	4	4	2	,,
4	4	4	4	1	,,
5	4	4	4	.	,,
6	4	4	3	4	,,
7	4	4	3	3	,,
8	4	4	3	2	,,
9*	4	4	3	1	,,
10	4	4	3	..	,,
11	4	4	2	4	,,
12	4	4	2	3	,,
13*	4	4	2	2	,,
14*	4	4	2	1	,,
15	4	4	2	.	,,
16	4	4	1	4	,,
17*	4	4	1	3	,,
18*	4	4	1	2	,,
19*	4	4	1	1	,,
20	4	4	1	.	,,

Form A 1 represents a stanza of 4 lines, each line containing 4 stress-units;—that is, an ordinary Romance stanza. In Form A 2, the last stress-unit of the fourth line has been dropped, so that the lines contain 4, 4, 4, and 3 units; an additional unit has been dropped in each of the succeeding forms A 3, A 4, and A 5,—the last-named leaving the stanza a simple triplet. In Form A 6, a unit has been dropped from the third line, and the same variations are repeated in Forms A 6 to A 10 as in Forms A 1 to A 5.

It will be observed that the progressive variations flow naturally from the typical first form A 1. Other forms arise when lines 3 and 4 are taken seriatim as lines 1 and 2; that is, when 4 3, 4 2, 4 1, etc. are substituted for the 4 4 of lines 1 and 2. The new series is represented by Aa, the various forms being represented by the addition of figures. Thus Aa2, 1 represents a stanza whose lines contain respectively 4 3 4 4 stress-units. The figure 2 following Aa represents lines 3 4 of the form A2, and the figure 1 represents lines 3 4 of the form A1. Again, the forms Aa2, 2, Aa 2, 3, Aa 2, 4, etc. represent stanzas of 4 3 4 3, 4 3 4 2, 4 3 4 1 stress-units; Aa6, 16 represents a stanza 3 4 1 4, Aa16, 6 a stanza 1 4 3 4, Aa6, 6 a stanza 3 4 3 4, Aa12, 3 a stanza 2 3 4 2, and so on. Thus the series opening Aa2 contains 20 forms, the 2 being followed by any of the numbers from 1 to 20; similarly Aa3 contains 20 forms, Aa4 20, and so on. That is, for the 4 4 of lines 1 and 2, the lines 4 3, or 4 2, or 4 1, etc. may be substituted from 1 to 20. The variations marked with an asterisk * are referred to on p. 210.

A second series arises on one of the lines being doubled:

B1	4 4 44 4	B21	4 4 34 4	B41	4 4 24 4	B61	4 4 14 4
2	4 4 44 3	22	4 4 34 3	42	4 4 24 3	62	4 4 14 3
3	4 4 44 2	23	4 4 34 2	43	4 4 24 2	63	4 4 14 2
4	4 4 44 1	24	4 4 34 1	44	4 4 24 1	64	4 4 14 1
5*	4 4 44 .	25*	4 4 34 .	45*	4 4 24 .	65*	4 4 14 .
6	4 4 43 4	26	4 4 33 4	46	4 4 23 4	66*	4 4 13 4
7	4 4 43 3	27	4 4 33 3	47	4 4 23 3	67*	4 4 13 3
8	4 4 43 2	28	4 4 33 2	48	4 4 23 2	68*	4 4 13 2
9*	4 4 43 1	29*	4 4 33 1	49*	4 4 23 1	69*	4 4 13 1
10*	4 4 43 .	30*	4 4 33 .	50*	4 4 23 .	70*	4 4 13 .
11	4 4 42 4	31	4 4 32 4	51*	4 4 22 4	71*	4 4 12 4
12	4 4 42 3	32	4 4 32 3	52*	4 4 22 3	72*	4 4 12 3
13*	4 4 42 2	33*	4 4 32 2	53*	4 4 22 2	73*	4 4 12 2
14*	4 4 42 1	34*	4 4 32 1	54*	4 4 22 1	74*	4 4 12 1
15*	4 4 42 .	35*	4 4 32 .	55*	4 4 22 .	75*	4 4 12 .
16	4 4 41 4	36*	4 4 31 4	56*	4 4 21 4	76*	4 4 11 4
17*	4 4 41 3	37*	4 4 31 3	57*	4 4 21 3	77*	4 4 11 3
18*	4 4 41 2	38*	4 4 31 2	58*	4 4 21 2	78*	4 4 11 2
19*	4 4 41 1	39*	4 4 31 1	59*	4 4 21 1	79*	4 4 11 1
20*	4 4 41 .	40*	4 4 31 .	60*	4 4 21 .	80*	4 4 11 .

In Series B the third line is doubled, and the full
variations of the series are obtained by taking lines
3 and 4 of Series A as lines 1 and 2, and adding lines
3 and 4 of Series B. Thus the table as arranged shews
the variations resulting from combining A 1 and B 1
to 80: these various forms are represented by B 1, 1,
B 1, 2, B 1, 67 etc., where the first figure represents
lines 3 and 4 of A, the second lines 3 and 4 of B. Thus:

B	2,	2	represents	4	3	44 3
B	11,	7	„	2	4	43 3
B	16,	16	„	1	4	41 4

Series Ba has the first line doubled instead of the third,
and is obtained by taking lines 3 and 4 of Series B,
followed by lines 3 and 4 of Series A. Thus:

Ba	2,	2	represents	44	3	4 3
Ba	11,	7	„	42	4	3 3
Ba	47,	16	„	23	3	1 4

Series Bb has both the first and the third lines doubled,
and is obtained by taking lines 3 and 4 of B and using
them alternately as lines 1 and 2, and 3 and 4. Thus:

Bb	2,	2	represents	44	3	44 3
Bb	11,	7	„	42	4	43 3
Bb	47,	16	„	23	3	41 4

These are common forms: less common ones follow.

Series Bc has the second line doubled, and is obtained
by taking lines 3 and 4 of Series B as lines 2 and 1,
not 1 and 2, and lines 3 and 4 of Series A as lines 3
and 4. Thus:

Bc	2,	2	represents	3	44	4 3
Bc	11,	7	„	4	42	3 3
Bc	16,	16	„	4	41	1 4
Bc	47,	16	„	3	23	1 4

Series Bd has the fourth line doubled, and is obtained by taking lines 3 and 4 of Series A as lines 1 and 2, and lines 3 and 4 of Series B as lines 4 and 3. Thus:

Bd	2,	2 represents	4	3	3	44
Bd 11,	7	„	2	4	3	43
Bd 16,	16	„	1	4	4	41
Bd 16,	67	„	1	4	3	13

Series Be has both the second and the fourth lines doubled, and is obtained by taking lines 3 and 4 of Series B alternately as lines 2 and 1, and 4 and 3. Thus:

Be	2,	2 represents	3	44	3	44
Be 11,	7	„	4	42	3	43
Be 47,	16	„	3	23	4	41

Series Bf has lines 1 and 2 doubled, and is obtained by taking lines 3 and 4 of Series B alternately as 1 and 3, and 2 and 4. Thus:

Bf	2,	2 represents	44	44	3	3
Bf 11,	7	„	42	43	4	3
Bf 47,	16	„	23	41	3	4

Series Bg has lines 2 and 3 doubled, and is obtained by taking lines 3 and 4 of Series B alternately as lines 2 and 1, and 3 and 4. Thus:

Bg	2,	2 represents	3	44	44	3
Bg 11,	7	„	4	42	43	3
Bg 47,	16	„	3	23	41	4

Series Bh has lines 3 and 4 doubled, and is obtained by taking lines 4 and 3 of Series B alternately as lines 1 and 3, and 2 and 4. Thus:

Bh	2,	2 represents	3	3	44	44
Bh 11,	7	„	4	3	42	43
Bh 47,	16	„	3	4	23	41

Series Bi has lines 1 and 4 doubled, and is obtained by taking lines 3 and 4 of Series B alternately as lines 1 and 2, and 4 and 3. Thus:

Bi	2,	2	represents	44	3	3	44
Bi	11,	7	„	42	4	3	43
Bi	47,	16	„	23	3	4	41

Series Bj has three lines doubled, lines 1, 2, and 3; and is obtained by using the various forms of line 3, Series B, as lines 1 and 2, and following with lines 3 and 4 of Series B. Thus:

Bj	2,	2,	2 represents	44	44	44	3
Bj	11,	7,	4 „	42	43	44	1
Bj	47,	16,	23 „	23	41	34	2

Series Bk has lines 1, 2, and 4 doubled, and is obtained by using the various forms of line 3, Series B, as lines 1 and 4, and lines 3 and 4, Series B, as lines 2 and 3. Thus:

Bk	2,	2,	2 represents	44	44	3	44
Bk	11,	7,	4 „	42	44	1	43
Bk	47,	16,	23 „	23	34	2	41

Series Bl has lines 1, 3, and 4 doubled, and is obtained by using lines 3 and 4, Series B, as lines 1 and 2, and the various forms of line 3, Series B, as lines 3 and 4. Thus:

Bl	2,	2,	2 represents	44	3	44	44
Bl	11,	7,	4 „	42	4	43	44
Bl	47,	16,	23 „	23	3	41	34

Series Bm has lines 2, 3, and 4 doubled, and is obtained by using lines 3 and 4, Series B, as lines 2 and 1 respectively, and the various forms of line 3, Series B, as lines 3 and 4. Thus:

Bm	2,	2,	2 represents	3	44	44	44
Bm	11,	7,	4 „	4	42	43	44
Bm	47,	16,	23 „	3	23	41	34

There may be a Series Bn, where all four lines are doubled, but unless the rime absolutely indicates this, the stanza will resolve into other and simpler forms. For instance, in Beaumont and Fletcher's *Nice Valour*, or *Passionate Madman*, occurs a song on Melancholy, whose first stanza is:

> Hence, all you vain delights,
> As short as are the nights
>   Wherein you spend your folly;
> There's nought in this life sweet,
> If wise men were to see't,
>   But only Melancholy,
>   O, sweetest Melancholy!

There is no doubt that here the last line is doubled: the line "O, sweetest Melancholy!" may be omitted, and the stanza is then on the ordinary Dowsabel pattern, where the first and third lines are doubled. The second line of the above may be doubled in the same way as is the fourth:

> Hence, all you vain delights,
> As short as are the nights
>   Wherein you spend your folly,
>   O, false-envisaged Folly!
> There's nought in this life sweet,
> If wise men were to see't,
>   But only Melancholy,
>   O, sweetest Melancholy!

The rime now may reveal that a doubling has taken place in all lines; but were the feminine rimes made ordinary, simple couplets would result; and in the second and third stanzas the above song does so resolve into couplets.

It will be much simpler, then, and indeed more in accord with natural formation, to consider three as the greatest number of lines that may be regarded as doubled in a two-versed stanza: are all four doubled, the stanza becomes a four-versed couplet-stanza,—so that through excess of complexity the poet slips again into simplicity.

A third Series, C, arises when the third line is trebled:

C	1	4	4	444	4
	2	4	4	444	3
	3	4	4	444	2
	4	4	4	444	1
	5	4	4	444	.
	6	4	4	443	4
....					
	80	4	4	411	.

It will be observed that this is the same as Series B, except that the third line has an additional 4 prefixed. The forms of Series C number 320.

C	81	4	4	344	4
....					
	160	4	4	311	.
	161	4	4	244	4
....					
	240	4	4	211	.
	241	4	4	144	4
....					
	320	4	4	111	.

Each set of 80 is the same as Series B; a 3, 2, or 1 being prefixed to line 3.

The 4 is prefixed in forms from 1 to 80: the 3 in forms from 81 to 160: the 2 in forms from 161 to 240: the 1 in forms from 241 to 320.

The Series C to Cm runs parallel with the Series B to Bm, one or more lines being trebled instead of doubled.

A fourth Series, BC and its reverse CB, combine Series B and C: that is, one line is doubled, and one trebled.

Series BC has line 1 doubled and line 3 trebled, and is obtained by taking lines 3 and 4 of Series B as lines 1 and 2, followed by lines 3 and 4 of Series C: the reverse is obtained by taking lines 3 and 4 of Series C as lines 1 and 2, followed by lines 3 and 4 of Series B. Thus:

BC	2,	2	represents	44	3	444	3
BC	11,	7	„	42	4	443	3
BC	47,	16	„	23	3	441	4
BC	51,	216	„	22	4	241	4
CB	2,	2	„	444	3	44	3
CB	11,	7	„	442	4	43	3
CB	47,	16	„	423	3	41	4
CB	216,	51	„	241	4	22	4

Series BCa has line 2 doubled and line 3 trebled, and is obtained by taking lines 3 and 4 of Series B as lines 2 and 1, followed by lines 3 and 4 of Series C: the reverse is obtained by taking lines 3 and 4 of Series C as lines 2 and 1, followed by lines 3 and 4 of Series B. Thus:

BCa	2,	2	represents	3	44	444	3
BCa	11,	7	„	4	42	443	3
BCa	47,	16	„	3	23	441	4
BCa	51,	216	„	4	22	241	4
CBa	2,	2	„	3	444	44	3
CBa	11,	7	„	4	442	43	3
CBa	47,	16	„	3	423	41	4
CBa	216,	51	„	4	241	22	4

Series BCb has line 4 doubled and line 3 trebled, and is obtained by taking lines 3 and 4 of Series B as lines 4 and 1, and lines 3 and 4 of Series C as lines 3 and 2: the reverse by taking lines 3 and 4 of Series C as lines 4 and 1, and lines 3 and 4 of Series B as lines 3 and 2. Thus:

BCb	2,	2 represents	3	3	444	44
BCb	11,	7 "	4	3	443	42
BCb	47,	16 "	3	4	441	23
BCb	51,	216 "	4	4	241	22
CBb	2,	2 "	3	3	44	444
CBb	11,	7 "	4	3	43	442
CBb	47,	16 "	3	4	41	423
CBb	216,	51 "	4	4	22	241

Series BCc has line 1 doubled and line 2 trebled, and is obtained by taking lines 3 and 4 of Series B as lines 1 and 3, and lines 3 and 4 of Series C as lines 2 and 4: the reverse by taking lines 3 and 4 of Series C as lines 1 and 3, and lines 3 and 4 of Series B as lines 2 and 4. Thus:

BCc	2,	2 represents	44	444	3	3
BCc	11,	7 "	42	443	4	3
BCc	47,	16 "	23	441	3	4
BCc	51,	216 "	22	241	4	4
CBc	2,	2 "	444	44	3	3
CBc	11,	7 "	442	43	4	3
CBc	47,	16 "	423	41	3	4
CBc	216,	51 "	241	22	4	4

Series BCd has line 1 doubled and line 4 trebled, and is obtained by taking lines 3 and 4 of Series B as lines 1 and 2, followed by lines 3 and 4 of Series C as lines 4 and 3; the reverse by taking lines 3 and 4

of Series C as lines 1 and 2, followed by lines 3 and 4
of Series B as lines 4 and 3. Thus:

BCd	2,	2	represents	44	3	3	444
BCd	11,	7	„	42	4	3	443
BCd	47,	16	„	23	3	4	441
BCd	51,	216	„	22	4	4	241
CBd	2,	2	„	444	3	3	44
CBd	11,	7	„	442	4	3	43
CBd	47,	16	„	423	3	4	41
CBd	216,	51	„	241	4	4	22

Series BCe has line 2 doubled and line 4 trebled,
and is obtained by taking lines 3 and 4 of Series B as
lines 2 and 1, and lines 3 and 4 of Series C as lines 4
and 3: the reverse by taking lines 3 and 4 of Series C
as lines 2 and 1, and lines 3 and 4 of Series B as lines
4 and 3. Thus:

BCe	2,	2	represents	3	44	3	444
BCe	11,	7	„	4	42	3	443
BCe	47,	16	„	3	23	4	441
BCe	51,	216	„	4	22	4	241
CBe	2,	2	„	3	444	3	44
CBe	11,	7	„	4	442	3	43
CBe	47,	16	„	3	423	4	41
CBe	216,	51	„	4	241	4	22

There may be occasional stanzas where more than
one line may be doubled and one trebled, or more than
one trebled and one doubled; they will be found of
extremely rare occurrence, however, and may be
grouped together until necessity calls for separate
groups, when they are easily prepared. They may
follow on as BCf, etc., or as 2BC, indicating two lines
doubled and one trebled, and 3BC, indicating three

doubled, or 2B2C, indicating two doubled and two trebled, etc.

A fourth Series, D, arises when a line is quadrupled; but this occurs in such small variety that it is simply indicated. In its simple form it would, of course, have 1220 variations, all based on C as those of C are based on B; it would also have the various combinations with doubled and trebled lines that C has with doubled lines.

The foregoing tables shew in detail the progression of variation possible in four-lined lyric stanzas, Romance, Ballad, Nibelungen, and Alexandrine. The numbers 4 4 4 4, 4 4 4 3, etc., represent the number of units in each line occupied with sound. It will be seen that there is a regular progression in the variations from 1 to 20: Nos. 5, 10, 15, and 20 are simply triplets. It does not mean that in every instance of triplets a line has been dropped, but simply that a triplet naturally falls into this place in the scheme, where the last line gradually drops a stress,—4, 3, 2, 1, 0.

There are several variations which, whilst they may and do exist theoretically, do not exist actually: these are marked with an asterisk *. The variations A 9, 13, and 17 practically resolve into variation 5; for 4 4 3 1, 4 4 2 2, and 4 4 1 3 are each equivalent to 4 4 0:

4	Bright scenes where boyhood's years were spent,
4	Where youth found little discontent,—
3	With you I may not dwell;—
1	Farewell.
4	Thy form might I again behold,
4	Thy clear deep stedfast eyes of blue,—
2	That wonder too,
2	Thy hair of gold,—

4   There is a joy beyond delight,
4   There is a feeling beyond speech
1   The night
3   Of moonless stars shall teach.

These stanzas, whilst they may, in Hesperidean fashion, be so printed, are nothing more than triplets, and are as well printed, so far as natural formation goes,—

4   Bright scenes where boyhood's years were spent,
4   Where youth found little discontent,—
4   With you I may not dwell;—Farewell.

4   Thy form might I again behold,
4   Thy clear deep stedfast eyes of blue,—
4   That wonder, too, thy hair of gold,—

4   There is a joy beyond delight,
4   There is a feeling beyond speech
4   The night of moonless stars shall teach.

Similarly, Forms A 14 and 18 are printed variants of Form 10, and Form 19 of Form 15. The following is an example of Form 19:

4   The days whose hours are budding flowers
4   Wherewith Time decks his paramours,—
1   Alas!
1   They pass;

and it resolves into:

4   The day whose hours are budding flowers
4   Wherewith Time decks his paramours,—
2   Alas! they pass;

where a slight hover only may divide "Alas!" and "They pass," or a pause equal to a full unit. Again, the Form Aa 19, 19,—1, 1, 1, 1, may at first sight appear an impossible, or at least an improbable form: yet the following are actual examples:

Out of sight,
    Out of mind!
Could the light
    Prove unkind?

Can the sun
    Quite forget
What was done
    Ere he set?
(A. Swinburne, *A dark Month*,
    No. 18, st. 1, 2.)

When I go
    From my place
At your feet,
    Sweet,

All I know
    Of your face
I recall—
    All;
(A. Dobson, *To F. M. D.*)

These poems really resolve into couplets, independently riming:

Out of sight, out of mind! Could the light prove unkind?
Can the sun quite forget what was done ere he set?

and

When I go from my place at your feet, sweet,
All I know of your face I recall—all.

The form Aa 14, 9,—2, 1, 3, 1, likewise has the example:

Because I adore you
    And fall
On the knees of my spirit before you—
    After all

You need not insult,
    My king,
With neglect, though your spirit exult
    In the spring.
(A. Swinburne, *A dark Month*, No. 19, st. 1, 2.)

This resolves into the form Aa 6,—the couplet 3, 4:

Because I adore you and fall
On the knees of my spirit before you—after all

You need not insult, my king,
With neglect, though your spirit exult in the spring.

These resolutions become more numerous as the stanza-forms become more unusual. For instance; in

Series B, Forms 36, 37, 38, and 39; 51, 52, 53, and 54; 66, 67, 68, and 69, simply resolve into Forms 1, 2, 3, and 4 of Series A:

$$\begin{rcases} \begin{matrix} 4 & 4 & 31 & 4 \\ 4 & 4 & 31 & 3 \\ 4 & 4 & 31 & 2 \\ 4 & 4 & 31 & 1 \end{matrix} \end{rcases} = \begin{cases} \begin{matrix} 4 & 4 & 22 & 4 \\ 4 & 4 & 22 & 3 \\ 4 & 4 & 22 & 2 \\ 4 & 4 & 22 & 1 \end{matrix} \end{cases} = \begin{cases} \begin{matrix} 4 & 4 & 13 & 4 \\ 4 & 4 & 13 & 3 \\ 4 & 4 & 13 & 2 \\ 4 & 4 & 13 & 1 \end{matrix} \end{cases} = \begin{cases} \begin{matrix} 4 & 4 & 4 & 4 \\ 4 & 4 & 4 & 3 \\ 4 & 4 & 4 & 2 \\ 4 & 4 & 4 & 1 \end{matrix} \end{cases}$$

Variations 5, 10, 15, and 20 of Series B are palpably the same as Forms 1, 2, 3, and 4 of Series A.

In Series B, the third line is doubled. Variations 1 to 20 are the same as in Series A, except that the third line is doubled;—that is, if a 4 be prefixed to the figures of the third line of Series A, Forms 1 to 20 of Series B result. Similarly, Forms 21 to 40, 41 to 60, and 61 to 80 of Series B, are produced by prefixing a 3, 2, or 1 respectively, to the figures of the third line of Series A. This is the common form of the Christabelle stanza.

The second form of the Christabelle stanza, where the first instead of the third line is doubled, results when lines 3 and 4 of Series B are taken as lines 1 and 2, and followed by lines 3 and 4 of Series A. This becomes Series Ba. It is a form used much less frequently than B, and it takes less variation, whilst theoretically it admits as much. If the second member of the doubled line drop a unit, becoming 43 4 4 4, the grouping is inclined to become 4 3 44 4;—that is, the doubling is inclined to take place in the *third* line instead of the first. The stanza

> I wandered in a lonely glade
>   Where issued from the shade
> A little murmuring mountain stream;
>   Along the winding vale it play'd
> Beneath the cloudless morning beam

flows much more naturally as:

> I saw where in a lonely glade
>   A little mountain stream
> Came wandering from the forest shade;
> Along the winding vale it play'd
>   Beneath the cloudless morning beam.

It would flow yet more naturally were the word "cloudless" omitted from the last line, and were the pause at "stream" made more pronounced:

> I saw within a lonely glade
>   A little mountain stream;
> It wandered from the forest shade,
> Along the winding vale it play'd
>   Beneath the morning beam.

and it flows almost as naturally as the poet wrote it:

> I wandered in a lonely glade,
> Where issuing from the forest shade,
>   A little mountain stream
> Along the winding valley play'd
>   Beneath the morning beam.
>
> (J. Montgomery, *A walk in Spring*, st. 1.)

The chief unnaturalness in the stanza as first quoted appears to be the coupling of the uneven lines with rime. Though such coupling may be met with, it is met with comparatively seldom. A second unnaturalness, if here a minor one, is in the unusual distribution of the thought in three lines of which the *second* is the short line;—usually the thought ends with a short line. Nothing is being urged against a stanza such as this; an attempt is merely being made to explain the rarity of its occurrence.

The Series Bb includes the joyous Dowsabel stanza. It is, of course, no more than a combination of Series

B and Ba, and it is far more frequently used than either of those two.

The remaining varieties of the Series,—Bc to Bm, where the other lines are doubled, are of rare occurrence, and their occurrence is more frequent in Romance than in Ballad stanzas.

There is far greater irregularity in the doubling of Romance lines than in the doubling of Ballad lines: 44 3 is a doubling without doubt; 44 4 is dubious: it may be a couplet and half a couplet. Indeed, it is probable that there was no doubling in Romance until after the doubling in the Ballad had become well established. In Romance a doubling and a couplet produce the same result; in Ballad it is quite different. Yet an examination of stanzas shews that a parallel doubling has consciously taken place in the two forms, stanzas being built on a similar model; but since Romance lacked the clear guide of the Ballad,—the short line,—there was a tendency towards confusion in the Romance form. Romance is at its best in couplet and cross-riming; Ballad is as excellent in these, but also revels in complicated doubling, trebling, and rime-weaving, producing isolated gems, or ropes and chains of charming Hesperidean jewel-melodies.

The third great Series, C, runs parallel with Series B:

Series B	4	4	44	4	Series C		4	4	444	4
Ba,	44	4	4	4	Ca,	444	4	4	4	
Bb,	44	4	44	4	Cb,	444	4	444	4	
Bc,	4	44	4	4	Cc,	4	444	4	4	
Bd,	4	4	4	44	Cd,	4	4	4	444	
Be,	4	44	4	44	Ce,	4	444	4	444	

etc.

As Series B passes through 80 forms, so Series C passes through 320, four series being produced by prefixing to line 3 first a 4, then a 3, then a 2, then a 1. Again, there is a further series produced by the mingling of doubled and trebled lines,—a mingling of Series B and C; so that in addition to the above there are:

Series BC	44		4	444		4		Series CB	444		4	44		4
BCa,		4	44	444		4		CBa,		4	444	44		4
BCb,		4		4	444	44		CBb,		4	4		44	444
BCc,	44	444		4		4		CBc,	444	44		4		4
BCd,	44		4		4	444		CBd,	444		4		4	44
BCe,		4	44		4	444		CBe,		4	444		4	44

There are occasional stanzas where three lines, or more, are doubled or trebled:

> The vision comes at deep midnight,
> When earth lies sleeping in starlight,
> And wraiths arise in wreaths of white
>   Where alder-marged and still,
>   The lakelet meets the hill;
> For thoughts swim up and make escape,
> And in the floating wraiths take shape
>   Whether or no I will.

Such stanzas are exceptional, but it is evident that they are possible.

As the Series advance, fewer and fewer of the possible variations are used; and these Tables of forms are simply intended to shew that, enormous as the number of possible variations may be, the whole of these flow in a natural and ever-broadening sequence from one primitive and fundamental natural form.

It will be found that the great bulk of lyric poetry can be classified, on the scheme of the foregoing verse-forms and stanza-forms, as naturally as flowers can be classified botanically; and the inference is that poems are natural efflorescences of thought, following definite laws like other efflorescences.

Odic stanzas have not been included,—that is, stanzas where heroic verses are introduced. It has been seen that certain combinations of lyric and heroic shew some tendency to slip into another form that is purely lyric, so that the heroic apparently has some material connection with lyric,—but the writer confesses that so far this connection has eluded him.

An anthology has been prepared, based on the foregoing laws; but it is too comprehensive to be included in this volume.

INDEX

feet, classic, temporal value of, 56
feminine iamb, the amphibrach, 27, 47; double feminine, 28; in classification, 186–187, 192
fiddle banished ballad as dance accompaniment, 172
"fingering" of rhythm, 24,181–182
five-syllabled units, 32, 33, 34–35
Fond Lover stanza, 138
"foot," Saintsbury's use of term, 10–11; position of stress in, 20–21
four-syllabled rhythm, two kinds, 32 and on; variations in, 37; metamorphosis in, 41, 165; four-syllabled unit of Blank never makes rhythmical scheme, 54
fractional verses, 120

ghost-foot, 28
Goldsmith, O., *Stanzas on Woman*, 192
Gollancz, I., nine-syllabled verse, 117
Gordon, A. L., *The Romance of Britomart*, 191
Greene, P., variability of trochee, 22
Grundtvig, N. F. S., *Agnes and the Merman*, 125, 127
Guest, E., sections of, 8, 10; adjacent accents, 104–105

Harleian MS., song from, 150
heart-beat, as basis of time in music, and of stress-unit, 55; analysis of, 55
heavy units, 42, 49; in heroic couplet, 82; in blank verse, 101–104
Hemans, D. F., *Music of Yesterday*, 75; *Roman Girl's Song*, 90; *Owen Glyndwr's War-Song*, 152; *The Voice of Scio*, 153
Henryson, R., *Robin and Makyne*, 132
heroic couplet, 77; an intermediary form, 77; rules for, 79, 80; swell to lyric, 82–83; triplet, 82; lyric nature, 83–84; Ballad verse in, 83; conversion to Alexandrine, 84; intermediary between heroic

and lyric, 49–50, 85–89; heroic closing Alexandrine sonnet, 92; run-on form of h. c., 93; rimeless or end-stopped h. c., 96; blend of heroic and lyric, 164
Herrick, R., *To Anthea*, 132; *The Dirge of Jephtha's Daughter*,161; *Kissing Usurie*, 168; *To Music*, 169; *Comfort to a Youth*, 170; *His Recantation*, 170; *Upon his departure hence*, 171; *The Primrose*, 195
Hogg, J., *Highland Laddie*, 194
Horace, stanza form of *Odes*, 134–135
hovers in verse, 4, 9; in stress-unit, 17, 20, 44–49, 85–90, 100–108, 117; noted by Ruskin, 21; dividing words, 22; filling of, 62, 89; long pause where whole units are dropped, 163–164
Hunt, L., *O lovely age of gold*, 41; note on brace indicating triplet in heroic couplets, 83; Ballad verse in heroic, 84; *Captain Sword and Captain Pen*, 193; irregular verse, 193
Hyde, D., *My Love, oh she is my Love*, 131
hymns, metre of, 65

iamb, regarded as a temporal unit, 18; varying values, 19 and on; Ruskin's three kinds, 21; number of accents in, 42; heavy iamb, 42–43; light iamb, 43–44; feminine iamb, 27, 47; syllabic weight, 47; heart-beat an iamb, 55
iambic rhythm, reason for tilt from trochaic, 57
indentation indicating riming lines, 167
inversions in verse, 3; inversions of rhythm, 106
Irving Shakespeare, nine-syllabled verse, 114
isochronous interval of Patmore, 11

Jockey to the Fair stanza, 147
John Brown's body lies..., pauses in verses, 163–164

For EU product safety concerns, contact us at Calle de José Abascal, 56–1°,
28003 Madrid, Spain or eugpsr@cambridge.org.

www.ingramcontent.com/pod-product-compliance
Ingram Content Group UK Ltd.
Pitfield, Milton Keynes, MK11 3LW, UK
UKHW012331130625
459647UK00009B/204